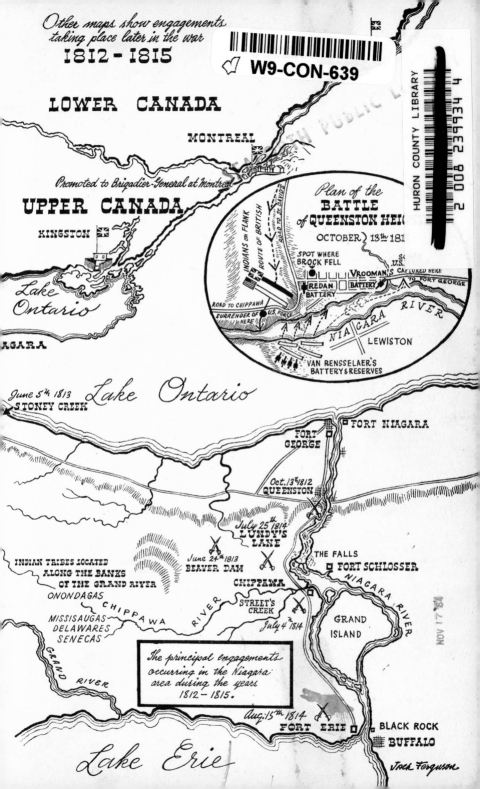

Other maps show engagements
taking place later in the war
1812 - 1815

LOWER CANADA

MONTREAL

Promoted to Brigadier-General at Montreal

UPPER CANADA

KINGSTON

Lake Ontario

AGARA

Plan of the
BATTLE
of QUEENSTON HEIG
OCTOBER 13th 181

INDIANS on FLANK
ROUTE of BRITISH
ROAD TO DAVIS

SPOT WHERE
BROCK FELL
VROOMAN'S CAPTURED HERE
S
U.S.
BATTERY
TO FORT GEORGE
REDAN
BATTERY

ROAD TO CHIPPAWA
SURRENDER OF U.S. FORCE
HERE

NIAGARA RIVER

LEWISTON

VAN RENSSELAER'S
BATTERY & RESERVES

June 5th 1813
STONEY CREEK

Lake Ontario

FORT
GEORGE
FORT NIAGARA

Oct.13th 1812
QUEENSTON

July 25th 1814
LUNDY'S
LANE

June 24th 1813
BEAVER DAM

THE FALLS
FORT SCHLOSSER

INDIAN TRIBES LOCATED
ALONG THE BANKS
OF THE GRAND RIVER
ONONDAGAS
MISSISSAUGAS
DELAWARES
SENECAS

CHIPPAWA

CHIPPAWA
RIVER

STREET'S
CREEK
July 4th 1814

NIAGARA RIVER

GRAND
ISLAND

GRAND
RIVER

The principal engagements
occurring in the Niagara
area during the years
1812 - 1815.

Aug.15th 1814
FORT ERIE
BLACK ROCK
BUFFALO

Lake Erie

Jack Ferguson

GREAT STORIES OF CANADA

THE GOOD SOLDIER

GREAT STORIES OF CANADA

Many other titles in preparation

GREAT STORIES OF CANADA

The Good Soldier

THE STORY OF ISAAC BROCK

By D. J. GOODSPEED

Illustrated by Jack Ferguson

TORONTO : 1964 : MACMILLAN

Library of Congress Catalogue Card No. 64-21439

PRINTED IN CANADA

Contents

THE GOOD SOLDIER

1. Some Early Adventures

EARLY one morning in the year 1791 seven men walked in single file along a narrow forest path near Bridgetown, the capital of the West Indian island of Barbados. All the men wore the scarlet tunics and white breeches of one of His Majesty's infantry regiments, and their white-plumed shakos and the gold lace and dark green facings on their uniforms showed them to be officers of the 49th Foot. They walked quickly and in silence, as though anxious to finish whatever task had brought them out of barracks at dawn.

They were making their way to a lonely forest glade, which they had selected because of its level floor of lush green grass. As the officers approached the glade, they could see that a strip of white sand gleamed through a cluster of palm trees at the far edge of the clearing. Beyond the sand the blue Caribbean Sea sparkled in the sunlight. Brightly coloured birds flitted from tree to tree, their cries sounding above the beat of the nearby surf.

The first man to enter the clearing was a little, strutting captain with an unpleasant smirk on his face. He strode across to the far side of the glade, where he stopped and began to take off his sword belt and scarlet coat. He was followed by two other officers whose downcast manner

9

and gloomy faces contrasted strangely with the captain's swagger.

A moment later four more officers appeared. One of them, the regimental surgeon, carried a sinister-looking black satchel of medical instruments. Another held a flat leather pistol case under his arm. These officers also had long faces and an air of melancholy – all except an exceptionally large man in the centre of the group who walked along quite cheerfully.

This young officer, whose name was Isaac Brock, stood well over six feet two inches in height and was broad in proportion. His fair, boyish face was calm and his bright blue eyes showed no trace of fear, although everyone else in the glade was sure that within the next five minutes he would be lying dead.

Isaac had already been a soldier for six years, although he was only twenty-one, but he had only recently joined the 49th Regiment on its station in the Barbados. Almost immediately after his arrival in Bridgetown he had discovered that the junior officers of the regiment were being terrorized by a certain captain who was one of the worst bullies and deadliest pistol shots in the British army. The captain had killed several men in duels, and had come to enjoy duelling for its own sake. He was quarrelsome and insulting in the mess, but no one any longer dared to call him to account. Glad to find a new-comer to torment, the captain had soon turned on Brock. At first, too, the big young man, with his pleasant, friendly manners and open face, had looked like easy game. When Isaac answered the captain politely and attempted to keep out of his way, this only convinced the bully that Isaac was afraid of him. He redoubled his insults, and, since Brock had never flinched from danger in his life, it was not long before a challenge was issued and accepted.

In those days when an officer and gentleman was challenged to a duel he had no choice but to accept. Otherwise he would have been branded a coward and disgraced for life. The system was a vicious one; it was changed not long afterwards, but at this time Brock had to be prepared to fight. His brother officers had warned him of the danger, telling him that the captain had never been known to miss with a duelling pistol at twelve paces, but Brock had only smiled and gone about his business.

Now it was the morning of the duel. The captain was already standing in his shirt-sleeves at the far side of the glade. The seconds were inspecting the pistols, and the surgeon was opening his satchel. Brock carefully took off his sword and his tunic; then, in response to the summons of the seconds, he and the captain walked out to the centre of the duelling-ground.

There the seconds formally asked Brock and the captain if they would not be reconciled. Both refused. The pistols were offered and the two duellists each accepted one. Then Brock spoke:

"Since I am so much larger than my opponent," he said, "and therefore a better target, I have decided that it would be unfair to fight at the usual twelve paces."

A sneer appeared on the captain's face. He thought that at the last moment Brock intended to back down and apologize.

Brock, however, took a linen handkerchief out of his pocket and handed it to one of the seconds.

"I am the injured party," he said, "and so I have the right to decide the terms of the duel. We will fire at each other across this handkerchief."

For a moment or two the captain failed to understand what was being suggested, but when the meaning of the words became clear to him the sneer disappeared from his face. He turned deadly pale and began to stutter and stammer. If the duellists were separated from each other by no more than a handkerchief when they fired, both would almost certainly be killed. Brock merely smiled at the captain's protests and maintained that he had every right to insist on duelling across the handkerchief if he wished. The captain flatly refused. It was certain death, he said. He wouldn't fight at all.

His seconds looked at him coldly and with contempt, then apologized to Brock for their principal's refusal to fight. They repacked the pistols and went back to the fort without the captain, who shortly afterwards resigned his commission and left the regiment.

The officers of the 49th were delighted to be rid of the bullying captain, but they were a good deal more surprised at the outcome of the duel than Brock was. He had been quite prepared to fire across the handkerchief if necessary, but he already knew enough about human nature to guess that the captain would probably refuse to fight on such terms. Two keynotes of Brock's character always were his boldness and his ability to understand how his opponents thought.

If the quarrelsome duellist had known Brock better he could have avoided disgrace. All his life Isaac Brock had trained himself to face danger bravely. It was as well that he did so, for when he had been born on the little island of Guernsey on October 6, 1769, he had come into a world soon to be shaken by revolutions and by long and terrible wars.

The Brock family had lived on Guernsey for generations, and many of them had made names for themselves as soldiers and sailors. Naturally enough, therefore, Isaac decided early in life that the army was the only career for him. He was his parents' eighth son (ultimately he had nine brothers and four sisters) and the family was a very close-knit and affectionate one. They were drawn even more closely together by their father's death in 1777, when Isaac was only eight. Two years later an older brother, Ferdinand, was killed at Bâton Rouge on the Mississippi River, fighting for the British in the American War of Independence.

Isaac's boyhood was spent mainly on Guernsey, and like most boys he was more interested in sport than in his studies. He fished and sailed and learned to ride a horse along the hilly bridle-paths of the island. Since he was exceptionally strong and determined, he soon became a champion swimmer and the best boxer for his age and weight in Guernsey, but it was not only because of his strength and size that his schoolfellows looked up to him. Isaac possessed a natural gentleness and kindliness that made him popular with all who knew him.

His family, however, felt that his education was being

neglected on Guernsey – there were so many more inter-
esting things to do than Latin verbs and mathematics – so
when he was eleven years old Isaac was sent away to
school, first to Southampton and then to Rotterdam in
Holland. In Rotterdam he learned to speak French fluent-
ly, an accomplishment that was to be most useful to him
in later life.

When he left Guernsey, Isaac turned into a good
scholar and developed a love of reading that stayed with
him until the day he died. Nevertheless, his heart was set
on becoming a soldier as so many of his ancestors had

been. His eldest brother, John, was a captain in the 8th Foot, and when Isaac was sixteen his family purchased him a commission as ensign in this regiment.

After five years with various garrisons in England, he was promoted to lieutenant. The following year he exchanged into the 49th Foot as a captain and joined that regiment in the Barbados. Unfortunately, a soldier's life in the West Indies in the eighteenth century was dull and unhealthy. The garrison had little to do but drill and build fortifications, while the outbreaks of fever killed more soldiers than died in war-time. One such pestilence struck the 49th Regiment in 1793, and Isaac Brock lay for a long while near to death. In all likelihood he would have died if it had not been for the care of his servant, Private Dobson, who nursed him back to health.

Although he recovered from the fever, Isaac was so

weak and ill that he had to return to England on sick leave. He took Dobson with him, and retained him for the rest of his life.

At the beginning of 1793 Britain was still at peace, and neither her government nor her people wished to have anything to do with foreign quarrels. The unsuccessful war against the American colonies that had ended only eleven years earlier was still fresh in everyone's mind. But although Britain was at peace, terrible things were happening on the continent of Europe. Revolution had broken out in France in 1789, when oppressed people had risen against the king and overthrown their government.

The leadership of the French Revolution had been taken over almost immediately by cruel and violent men. In the jails political prisoners were murdered; the king and queen and countless aristocrats were sent to the guillotine; and all France was soon living under a reign of terror. The French revolutionaries were not content with getting rid of their own king and plunging their own country into chaos, but declared themselves the enemies of all kings everywhere. Before long most of Europe was at war, and when French armies occupied Belgium and invaded Holland, the English prime minister, William Pitt, reluctantly joined the alliance against France.

For four years Isaac Brock remained in charge of the depot battalion of his regiment in England, recruiting and training the soldiers who were sent out as reinforcements to the 49th in Jamaica and the Barbados. During this time the war against France went badly. Both the Austrians and a British army under the Duke of York were defeated in Holland, and Britain lost 80,000 soldiers in the West Indies, most of them dying of fever but some being killed in putting down a revolt of Negro slaves who had been encouraged by French revolutionary ideas to fight for their freedom.

In 1795 Brock purchased his promotion to major. (This was the normal way of obtaining promotion in the British Army at this time, and the officer who could not raise the money to pay for his "step" was likely to remain in a junior position throughout his entire career. Isaac was given the money for his promotions by his brother William, a prosperous merchant in the City of London.) In 1797 the 49th Regiment at last came home to England, and Isaac, at the age of twenty-eight, was promoted to be its senior lieutenant-colonel.

In Brock's time officers in the British army and navy were extremely strict with their men. The discipline was often harsh and unjust, and even small mistakes and offences were frequently punished with astonishing severity. Soldiers and sailors were sometimes flogged almost to death with a long, thonged whip called a "cat-o'-nine-tails" which was often dipped in salt and water so that every cut burned like fire. As a result, only the very poor and desperate who had no other way of making a living joined the army in the ranks. The navy found it even harder to get recruits, for the discipline there was crueller than in the army and the sailors often had to live at sea for months on end, eating only mouldy biscuits and wormy salt pork. The navy recruited in the prisons and the slums, and, when even these places of despair failed to provide enough men, press gangs were sent into the dock areas of Britain's great seaports to kidnap merchant seamen and force them aboard His Majesty's men-of-war.

In April and May of 1797 several mutinies broke out in the British navy. Ships' crews imprisoned their officers and sometimes tarred and feathered them before dumping them ashore; the red flag of revolt was run up to the mast-heads of most vessels of the fleet; the country was full of rumours that French secret agents were trying to corrupt the army and navy and stir them up to rebellion; and for several weeks the people of Britain feared that revolution might break out there just as it had in France. In the end the mutinies were suppressed, the ringleaders hanged, and the worst grievances of the men righted, but for the remainder of the year discipline in the navy remained shaky.

Some regiments of the army were also infected by the spirit of revolt, among them the 49th Foot, which was stationed on the banks of the Thames. The former commanding officer who had just been replaced by Brock had been unpopular, and the new colonel was not yet known to his men. Brock's first task, therefore, was to restore the discipline of his regiment.

He set about this with his usual common sense. When he took over the command his soldiers were on the point of open rebellion: men went about their duties sullenly and resentfully, and insolent slogans were chalked up on all the barrack-room walls. For nearly a month Colonel Brock remained awake each night, personally visiting the men's quarters and making sure that no conspiracies were being hatched. During this period he rarely went to bed before daylight and he slept with a brace of loaded pistols beside him.

In addition, however, Brock saw to it that the regiment was run as it should be. Men were no longer savagely punished for minor offences; floggings ceased; and the soldiers found themselves being treated kindly but with firmness. Soon their sullen resentment quite disappeared, to be replaced by trust and affection, and the Commander-in-Chief, the Duke of York, happily remarked that "Lieutenant-Colonel Brock, from one of the worst, had made the 49th one of the best regiments in the service."

In the cold, wet summer of 1799 the British government decided to invade Holland in order to liberate it from the French. The Royal Navy was to carry a Russian army from the Baltic to assist in the invasion, and it was hoped that the Dutch would rise against their oppressors. Because it had now been brought to such a high state of efficiency, Colonel Brock's regiment was chosen to serve in the expedition. Isaac's high-spirited younger brother, Savery, who had been forced to leave the navy because he had objected to a brutal punishment, accompanied the 49th to Holland as its paymaster.

The British force sailed in the middle of August, but south-westerly gales off the coast of Holland prevented a landing for two weeks. At last the troops were put ashore on the Helder, a barren peninsula of wind-swept sand-dunes north of Amsterdam.

The campaign in Holland went badly for the British. The British general in command advanced timidly inland; the weather was abominable, with rain and gusty winds; the soldiers often had nothing but sodden biscuits to eat; the French fought skilfully; and the Dutch made no move to support their liberators. Brock's regiment was not heavily engaged with the enemy until October 2, but when they finally met the French at Egmont-op-Zee they gave a good account of themselves.

"For my own part," Isaac wrote to his brother John, "I have every reason to be satisfied with the conduct of both officers and men, and no commanding officer could be more handsomely supported than I was on that day, ever glorious to the 49th."

Brock himself displayed the reckless daring that was typical of him. Perhaps because he was a big, strong man who was good at everything he ever put his hand to, Brock never seemed to take danger seriously. In the course of the Battle of Egmont-op-Zee his pistol holsters were shot away. He continued to expose himself to the hottest enemy fire, however, and towards the end of the day a spent musket-ball struck him on the throat and threw him off his horse. He was saved from death only by the fact that he was wearing a heavy cotton muffler around his neck over a thick silk scarf. The musket-ball went through both the muffler and the scarf but did not enter his neck. Brock remained on the field directing his men and did not even report the incident.

Young Savery Brock also distinguished himself that day. He had no intention of remaining out of the fight merely because he was paymaster, so he served his brigade commander as a dispatch-rider. When there were no

messages for him to carry, Savery light-heartedly took his place with the front-line troops. At one point in the battle Isaac saw his brother in the thick of the fighting and called out to him:

"By the Lord Harry, Master Savery! Did I not order you to stay with your iron chest unless you remained with the general? Go back to it, sir, immediately!"

But Savery only laughed and replied: "Mind your regiment, Master Isaac. You don't want me to quit the field now, do you?"

This exchange took place in front of the troops, who were delighted. For months afterwards they never tired of telling how their colonel and his brother had both been in the forefront of the battle that day.

The gallantry of the soldiers, however, could not make up for the timidity of the generals. Early in November the British and Russian forces re-embarked on their transports and sailed for England. They landed at Yarmouth, where the Russians amazed the townspeople by drinking the oil out of the street lamps, and soon afterwards the 49th Regiment was posted to the island of Jersey.

Colonel Brock was too good a soldier to complain about his superiors, even when he was writing to his brothers, but he was probably as disgusted with the result of the Dutch expedition as most men in the army. His experience in Holland confirmed him in his belief that a commander should be bold and daring rather than timid and cautious.

On coming back from Holland, Isaac Brock went on leave for a spell, leaving the regiment under the command of his junior, Lieutenant-Colonel Roger Sheaffe. Colonel Sheaffe was a believer in old-fashioned methods of discipline, and the men detested him. The first day after Brock returned from leave, the regiment was drawn up in review order on morning parade. When the men saw him they broke into spontaneous cheers. This apparent compliment to Brock displeased him. He reproved the men for their unmilitary conduct, marched them back to their barracks, and stopped all their leave for a week.

By now Napoleon Bonaparte, a brilliantly successful young general in the French army, had made himself dictator of France. His military genius was to enable France to fight single-handed against the whole of Europe for the next fifteen years. When Colonel Brock returned to his regiment from leave, England found herself alone in the war, for both the Austrians and the Russians had been forced to make peace.

Worse than this, the half-mad Tsar Paul of Russia, enraged at the defeat of his soldiers in Holland, had become friends with Napoleon and had bullied Denmark into an alliance aimed at Britain. If the Russian and Danish fleets sailed to join those of France, the Royal Navy would be outnumbered on the seas and Britain would have to surrender. Therefore the British government decided to send an expedition to Copenhagen. A fleet was fitted out under the command of Admiral Sir Hyde Parker, an elderly sailor who had little confidence in victory and who was nervous about "the dark nights and fields of ice" he might meet on the way to Copenhagen. Under Admiral Parker, however, as the naval second in command was

Lord Nelson, a one-eyed, one-armed little man who was the boldest, most spirited, and most brilliant sailor the world has ever seen. A body of troops was to accompany the expedition under Colonel Sir William Stewart, and Lieutenant-Colonel Isaac Brock went along as second in command with 760 men of his beloved 49th Regiment.

The soldiers embarked at Portsmouth on February 27, 1801, but, because Admiral Parker saw no reason to hurry, the flotilla did not sail until March 12. Twelve days later the British squadron dropped anchor in the Kattegat near Copenhagen. The Danes refused Admiral Parker's summons to surrender, but they delayed their reply long enough to strengthen their defences very greatly. Admiral Parker was in favour of sailing back to England, but Nelson coaxed his superior officer into giving him permission to attack with twelve ships of the line. Brock and the 49th Regiment were chosen to land and capture one of the principal Danish batteries.

The sea fight was so fierce, however, that no soldiers were put ashore. At one point in the battle Admiral Parker, watching with the rest of the fleet a few miles away, flew a signal ordering Nelson to break off the action and retire. Nelson turned to his captain and said: "You know, Foley, I have only one eye. I have the right to be blind sometimes." With this he put his telescope up to his blind eye and said: "I really do not see the signal. Keep mine for closer battle still flying. Nail it to the mast."

In response to Nelson's signal flags, the great white ships sailed closer in to the anchored Danish vessels, and soon the two fleets could scarcely be seen for the clouds of smoke from the English broadsides. One by one the Danish guns fell silent as Nelson's fire knocked them out. By two o'clock in the afternoon the Danish ships were smouldering wrecks, but the British too had been so badly battered that they could scarcely continue the fight. Nelson was really in a very dangerous position, for the Danish defences on shore were still unharmed. However, Nelson sent a confident summons to the Danish Crown Prince, who was commanding the Danish forces, urging him to consent to an armistice for the sake of humanity.

Nelson's bluff worked; the Danes agreed to suspend their alliance with England's enemies and to leave their warships unrepaired for fourteen weeks. Britain had retained command of the sea.

Colonel Brock, who had come aboard Nelson's flagship, the *Elephant,* towards the close of the battle and had seen the great admiral write his letter to the Crown Prince, had also observed how refusal to admit defeat could turn an apparently hopeless battle into a victory and how a timely ultimatum to a shaken enemy could bring unexpectedly cheap success.

When the 49th Regiment returned from Copenhagen it spent the winter in barracks in England, and in the spring of 1802 sailed for Canada. Colonel Brock sailed with it rather reluctantly. In Canada he would be far away from the great war against Napoleon. The only possible enemy in North America was the United States, which now had been at peace with Britain for almost twenty years. Brock did not like the thought of quiet garrison duty in a distant colony while so many of his brother officers would be winning glory in Europe.

The trip across the North Atlantic was stormy, but after being buffeted by high seas and driving winds Brock's ship at last found a quiet anchorage in the St. Lawrence River under the towering cliffs of Quebec.

The ancient capital had not changed much since Wolfe had captured it from the French forty-four years previously. Quebec was still surrounded by a high wall of grey stone, buttressed and embrasured for defence against a siege. Cannon muzzles still poked from this wall, aiming down at the river and covering the approaches to the fortress. On the cliff-top the ancient Château St. Louis still stood, scarred by the cannon-balls of earlier wars. Above the narrow streets of the Upper Town loomed the old cathedral, and just to the west of the cathedral was the Ursuline Convent where the wounded Montcalm had died after the Battle of the Plains of Abraham. From the anchorage Quebec looked far more like some ancient European city than like a colonial capital on the fringes of the wilderness.

Colonel Brock was not to stay long in Quebec. Out to the west, along the Great Lakes, stretched the 1,200-mile frontier between Canada and the United States. This frontier had to be guarded, and there were never enough soldiers for the task. Shortly after its arrival, the 49th Regiment was sent to do outpost duty in the province of Upper Canada.

2. The Suppression of a Mutiny

BROCK's regiment travelled from Quebec to Kingston by *bateaux* – the heavy, flat-bottomed river boats about twenty feet long and six feet wide that the French-Canadian *voyageurs* had developed for the St. Lawrence River. From Kingston the troops continued their journey by schooner, for, although a military road had been cut through the forest a few years before, no one travelled by this rough and bumpy route unless he had to.

At this time there were about 2,000 regular troops stationed in Lower Canada (now Quebec). In Upper Canada (Ontario), there were some 600-700 British soldiers. Neither province was thickly populated, but Lower Canada had 160,000 inhabitants as compared to only 14,000 in the upper province. Some Upper Canadian settlers were United Empire Loyalists who had left the United States after the American Revolution, but many of the inhabitants had come from the United States at a later date, attracted by the free land offered by the government. These later arrivals were often of doubtful loyalty, for many of them would have preferred to be American citizens.

Most of the 49th Regiment went into barracks at Fort

27

George near the present site of Niagara-on-the-Lake. Colonel Sheaffe was left in command at Fort George, and small detachments of soldiers, each under one or two officers, were posted at Fort Chippawa on the Niagara River a mile and a half above the falls, at Fort Erie, at Amherstburg on the western end of Lake Erie, and at Sandwich at the northern end of the Detroit River. Another British outpost, Fort Joseph, was manned at the head of Lake Huron. Colonel Brock remained at headquarters in the town of York, the capital of Upper Canada and the site of the present city of Toronto.

Even at the best of times life in these frontier garrisons was dull. The soldiers had little to do but drill, practise their musketry, and improve their fortifications. In their spare time they had no place to go for entertainment unless they were stationed near some small town where they could drink away their pay in the local tavern. During the long years of peace, it was easy for both officers and men to grow bored and restless.

Although Britain and the United States were at peace, there was little friendship between the two countries. The American War of Independence had been too recent for that. As a result, Americans who lived along the border encouraged British soldiers to desert.

"Why should you stay here in a miserable log fort in the forest?" they would whisper to the red-coats they met in the taverns. "If you came to the States you would be a free man. No more drill, no more parades, no more discipline."

A fair number of soldiers listened to this kind of talk,

broke their oath of enlistment, and slipped away across
the American border. Colonel Brock was not used to
commanding a regiment under such conditions, but he
had not been at Fort York long before he had to deal with
the problem.

One hot summer night in 1803, he was awakened by
his sergeant-major, James FitzGibbon, who reported that
three soldiers who should have been on sentry duty had
disappeared. A boat was also missing, and the sentry who
should have been guarding it was gone. Brock ordered
a roll-call to be held in the barracks. When the men had
tumbled out of their blankets to stand by their beds and
answer their names by lantern-light it was found that
three more soldiers of the 49th Regiment and a corporal
of the 41st were missing.

Colonel Brock at once decided to set out in pursuit of
the deserters. There was only one place they could have
gone: to Fort Niagara in the United States. Therefore
Brock immediately ordered the sergeant-major and twelve
men to prepare a *bateau* for a midnight journey across
the thirty miles of open lake that separated York from
Fort Niagara.

Brock divided his crew into two watches who rowed
turn and turn about for an hour each. Whenever there
was a breath of wind they hoisted the big square sail of
the *bateau*, but the night was calm and most of the time
they had to push the heavy boat along with the oars. To
encourage the men, Brock himself took regular turns at
rowing. His boyhood in Guernsey had made him thor-
oughly familiar with small boats, and the sight of his huge

figure bending to the oar was enough to make every member of the crew pull his hardest.

When they reached Fort George just after daylight, Brock sent out a detachment from the fort to scour the American side of the lake while he himself turned back towards York along the Canadian shore. The party from Fort George, under a Lieutenant Chesshire, took an Indian guide with them, and in the middle of the morning the Indian's sharp eyes spotted the scarlet coats of the deserters a long way off through the trees. After a chase of several miles the fugitives were all rounded up and arrested. The episode became the talk of the garrison, for no one could remember the lake ever being crossed in an open boat before. When the Commander-in-Chief heard of it, he was displeased, for he felt that Colonel Brock had run too great a risk.

In spite of his association with Isaac Brock, Colonel Sheaffe still had not learned how to handle men. Left to himself at Fort George, with Colonel Brock far away in York, Sheaffe had soon made himself unpopular with his soldiers. He frequently placed the little village of Niagara out of bounds and he insisted that no soldier was to leave the confines of the fort, even to fish in the river, unless he was properly dressed in scarlet tunic and spotless white trousers. The men were forbidden to use their muskets for hunting in the forest, even if they bought their own powder and shot. Thus, with a few simple regulations, Colonel Sheaffe ensured that his soldiers would have absolutely nothing to do in their leisure time. In addition, he handed out punishments freely, and the four "black holes" in the fort, where men were kept in solitary confinement on bread and water, were always full.

A group of soldiers decided they could no longer endure Colonel Sheaffe's discipline. Led by a Sergeant Clarke, a Corporal O'Brien, and a Private Rock (who had been a sergeant until his demotion earlier in the summer), these men planned to arrest all the officers of the garrison, lock them in the punishment cells, and then desert to the Americans. It was later claimed that they also intended to murder Colonel Sheaffe, and very probably some at least of the conspirators had resolved to do this, for they were desperate men who knew that they would be executed in any case if their plot failed. They planned to stage their mutiny some night when Sergeant Clarke and Corporal O'Brien were on guard duty together, and they held several meetings to work out the details.

The last of these meetings, which had been held in Knox's Tavern in Niagara, went on too long. One of the conspirators was late in returning to the fort for duty, and, as a result of a careless remark he made while hurrying to get on parade, Colonel Sheaffe's suspicions were aroused. Before long the officers of the garrison discovered a soldier who was willing to reveal the plot.

Colonel Sheaffe was appalled by what he discovered, for he knew how disastrous the consequences of a successful mutiny might be. If the officers at Fort George were imprisoned and their colonel killed, the original mutineers might well be joined by many more. The men were discontented and unhappy, and it was possible that most of the garrison might slip away across the border. Nor would the trouble end there. If one frontier fort were lost by mutiny, others might follow its example. That had been the pattern of the navy's mutiny in 1797. And if the British army in Canada were seriously weakened, the Americans might take the opportunity of attacking, in the hope of bringing all British North America under the United States flag.

Colonel Sheaffe felt that the situation was more than he could deal with alone. He called a secret meeting of all the officers at Fort George. They reported that the temper of the men was dangerous, that any small incident might set off serious trouble. In this predicament, Colonel Sheaffe and the officers decided that they needed the help of the one man who might be able to deal with the problem. They decided to send a report of the conspiracy to Colonel Brock at Fort York and to do nothing until they heard from him.

Fortunately there was a government schooner lying at anchor in the Niagara River that afternoon. Colonel Sheaffe at once wrote out a report and ordered the schooner to take it to York under full sail. Brock received Sheaffe's message that same evening.

Brock must have been dismayed to find that the happy, well-disciplined regiment he had brought to Canada only the previous year was once again endangered by the stupidity and harshness of some of its officers. But, although he had some secret sympathy with the mutineers, he had no doubt as to where his duty lay. The mutiny would have to be crushed before it began.

Brock did not hesitate a moment. Stopping only to pick

up his sergeant-major, he went down to the harbour and boarded the same schooner that had brought him Sheaffe's report.

"We must go back to Fort George," he told the schooner's captain, "as fast as your sails will carry us."

The return journey took longer, for the winds were against the little ship, and she had to tack back and forth across the lake, but Brock reached Niagara a little before noon the next day. He ordered the schooner to anchor below the village where he had a ship's boat set him ashore alone. Sergeant-Major FitzGibbon was told to remain out of sight below decks until sent for.

Colonel Brock then walked over to the fort by himself. The day was very hot, and since it was the soldiers' dinner hour no one was about. However, the sentry on the east gate recognized Brock's huge figure striding up to the fort.

"Turn out the guard!" the sentry shouted, coming smartly to attention and presenting arms. Out of the guardroom the guard came running, adjusting their uniforms as they came. They lined up in two ranks; the sergeant in charge called them to attention, then stepped out to salute the commanding officer.

As Colonel Brock looked the guard over, he realized that he had reached Fort George none too soon. This may have been the very day for which the mutineers had been waiting, for the sergeant of the guard was none other than Clarke and the corporal of the guard was O'Brien.

"Have your guard shoulder arms, sergeant," Brock said.

The muskets clattered and then the two ranks of soldiers stood rigid and motionless again.

"Come here, sergeant," Brock commanded, and the sergeant stepped out from his place to stand before the colonel. "Lay down your pike," Brock said. The sergeant hesitated for only an instant, although he must have guessed what was coming. Under the colonel's steady gaze he placed his pike on the ground.

"Take off your sword and sash and lay them down."

The sergeant again obeyed.

"Corporal O'Brien, bring a pair of handcuffs and put them on this sergeant."

The corporal doubled back into the guardroom and returned with the handcuffs. No one else moved. Colonel Brock, Sergeant Clarke, and all the members of the guard stood absolutely still under the hot summer sun.

The colonel spoke to the corporal again. "Lock the sergeant up in one of the cells and bring me the key."

Hastily the corporal did as he was told. When the sergeant was imprisoned, the corporal moved back to take up his place with the guard, but Brock was not yet finished.

"Come here, Corporal."

In a daze the corporal stepped out to stand where the sergeant had recently been.

"Lay down your arms and accoutrements," Brock commanded. When this had been done, the colonel spoke to the right-hand man of the guard. "Come here, you grenadier. Bring a pair of handcuffs, lock up this corporal in another cell, and bring me the key."

All was done as soon as the colonel ordered it. There was not a man who dared disobey.

"Drummer," Colonel Brock then ordered, "beat to arms."

A moment later the roll of the drum throbbed out across the grounds of the fort. Officers and men began to pour out of their barracks and mess-halls as they heard the urgent drumbeats from the east gate. The first officer to appear was a Lieutenant Williams, who came out of his quarters at the run, still buttoning his tunic and with his sword and belt clasped in his hand.

"Mr. Williams," Brock called out when he saw him, "go instantly and secure Private Rock. If he hesitates to obey, even for an instant, cut him down."

Williams saluted and went off at the run. In Rock's barrack-room the men were still putting on their tunics and shakos. The noise of the drum continued all the while, pounding out its note of urgency and alarm.

Lieutenant Williams called up the stairs for Private Rock to come down at once.

"Yes, sir," Rock replied, "as soon as I get my arms."

Williams went up the stairs two at a time. "I said 'come now'," Williams shouted. "Leave your arms."

"I must have my arms, sir," said Rock with a desperate glint in his eye. And he stretched out his hand to the musket rack, only to step back quickly when he found the point of the officer's sword against his chest.

"If you touch that musket, I'll cut you down," the lieutenant warned him, and Rock had no choice but to obey.

The rest of the mutineers were quickly rounded up and placed in irons. There were twelve of them all told, and they were herded together with the eight deserters Brock

had arrested in the United States a week or two before. The twenty prisoners were then placed aboard the schooner under a guard commanded by Sergeant-Major FitzGibbon and taken to York.

When this had been done, the garrison at Fort George
went back to its normal duties, but Colonel Brock was
not content to leave the matter there. He soon returned
to Fort George and announced to Colonel Sheaffe that

for the next few months he would remain and command in person.

The first thing Brock did was to remove the senseless restrictions Sheaffe had imposed. The soldiers were allowed to go to Niagara when they were off duty, provided only that they were properly dressed. Fishing was permitted in fatigue clothes, and Brock ruled that the men could hunt with their army muskets as much as they wished as long as they paid for their own powder and shot.

The change that came over the mutinous garrison at Fort George after Isaac Brock had been there for a little time was almost miraculous. The soldiers settled down contentedly to their work; there were no more attempts at desertion; and the four "black holes", which had always been full under Colonel Sheaffe, were empty.

There was, however, little mercy shown to the unfortunate men who had plotted rebellion. They were court-martialled in Quebec in September. Four of the mutineers, including Clarke, O'Brien, and Rock, and three of the deserters, were shot, but before they died they publicly declared that if they had continued under the command of Colonel Brock they would never have mutinied. One of the prisoners was pardoned because Brock spoke in his favour, but the remainder were all deported to the West Indies for life.

When the news of the executions reached Fort George, the entire garrison had to be paraded to hear the announcement read aloud, for this was the custom of the service. Colonel Brock was so affected by the fate of these men who had fought with him in Holland and at Copenhagen that he could hardly read the sentence aloud. His voice broke as he spoke to the regiment.

"Since I have had the honour to wear the British uniform I have never felt grief like this," he told the men. "It pains me to the heart to think that any member of my regiment should have engaged in a conspiracy which has led to their being shot like so many dogs . . ."

And all those on parade that day saw that Brock's cheeks were wet with tears as he spoke.

3. Strengthening the Defences of Lower Canada

THE winter of 1804 was long in the little army outpost in the Canadian bush. The Niagara River froze over and snow lay deep in the surrounding forest. Letters from York took more than a week to arrive, and letters from England ceased altogether until the spring.

Fort George itself was a low, square building made of logs and loopholed for musketry. Around the fort were earth ramparts and a cedar palisade which was neither high nor strong enough to be much defence against a determined assault. For several hundred yards on all sides of the palisade the forest and undergrowth had been cleared to provide a field of fire for the nine-pounders that were the fort's biggest guns.

The officers' quarters were rude but comfortable, and, on mess nights when the rough log walls lay in the shadows outside the pool of candlelight that illuminated the long table, it must almost have seemed as though the officers were dining in their regimental mess at home. White linen set off good china; crystal glasses and the regimental plate gleamed and sparkled; white-coated mess waiters stood behind the officers' chairs; the traditional toasts were proposed in the traditional way; the port decanter passed from right to left around the table; and, after the king's health had been drunk, the blue smoke of cigars curled up to the rough-hewn rafters.

That winter Colonel Brock, finding that he had time on his hands, turned to his books for pleasure and instruction. Although he had left school at sixteen, he had learned to love reading and through his own efforts had made himself a reasonably well-educated man.

In the near-by village of Niagara there was one man whom Brock came to know well that winter. Robert Nichol, a Scotsman who had come to Canada some years previously, kept the general store that supplied the little community with what few luxuries it had. He was a small, dark man with a sharp tongue and a very good opinion of himself, but, as Brock soon discovered, he was remarkably clever. Nichol became a frequent visitor to Fort George, where Brock often invited him to dine in the officers' mess. At first some of the officers raised their eyebrows at this, but when they saw their colonel so friendly with the little Scotsman they came to accept him. Brock liked Nichol for his own sake, but he also liked to talk to him about Upper Canada and thus improve his knowledge of the country. Before spring Brock had Nichol prepare a long report on the resources of the province, its roads, its waterways, and its population.

The Colonel was not the only one who spent much time in study that winter. Sergeant-Major FitzGibbon had served with Brock in Holland and Copenhagen and had so impressed him as a smart and brave young soldier that the Colonel decided to educate him so that some day he might qualify for a commission. With the kindness that was so natural to him, Brock lent FitzGibbon his own books and coached him in his studies to such good effect that the sergeant-major later became an officer and rose to the rank of colonel.

Nevertheless, Brock could be stern even with those to whom he was kindest. Once when he asked FitzGibbon why some order had not been carried out, the sergeant-major replied that it had been impossible. Brock was at once angry.

"By the Lord Harry, sir!" he said. "Do not tell me it is impossible! Nothing should be impossible to a soldier! The word impossible should not be found in a soldier's dictionary!"

The next year Brock returned to Quebec and was promoted to the rank of full colonel. That October he went on leave to England where he spent some time visiting his family. His eldest brother, John, a lieutenant-colonel in the 81st Foot, had been killed in a duel at the Cape of Good Hope, but the remainder of his brothers and sisters were all well. William was prospering as a London merchant, Daniel was an important man on the island of Guernsey, and young Savery, for whom Isaac had a special fondness, was in the army, serving with General Sir John Moore.

While he was in England on leave, Brock submitted a report to the British commander-in-chief, recommending the raising of a regiment of veterans for service in Canada. At the end of their term of enlistment, the veterans would each be given a grant of 200 acres of good land, and Brock believed that this would induce them to settle down in the country in a way that the soldiers of the regular regiments rarely did. Brock hoped that, if his suggestions were adopted, Canada might some day be defended in large part by such veteran soldiers and the ever-present problem of desertion on the frontier would cease to exist. The Duke of York received the report kindly, and the 10th Royal Veteran Battalion was sent to Canada the following year.

Before long, however, Brock began to find that the idleness of leave bored him. The war with France was going badly, and Napoleon, who by now had crowned himself Emperor of the French, was sweeping everything before him on the continent of Europe. For a time that summer it had even appeared as though England herself might be in danger. Napoleon had encamped on the Channel coast with a huge and powerful army that could easily have conquered England if only it could have been carried across the few miles of the Narrow Seas. Admiral Nelson had frustrated this plan when he utterly defeated the French fleet at the great naval battle of Trafalgar, but even before this Napoleon had abandoned his hopes of invading England. He had marched his Grand Army away from the Channel to defeat in turn each of England's allies on the Continent. An Austrian army had surrendered at Ulm, and a few weeks later Napoleon had badly beaten a combined Russian and Austrian army at Austerlitz. When the news of this battle had been reported to the English prime minister, William Pitt, he had realized that the war would be a long one.

"Roll up that map of Europe," Pitt said sadly. "We'll not need it again for ten years."

As the fortunes of France grew continuously brighter, the enemies of England in the United States became more and more outspoken, and many Americans openly advocated invading Canada. They remembered that France had helped the United States in its Revolutionary War against England, and many of them felt that the American Revolution was not really complete as long as any part of North America was under the British crown. By June of 1806 the situation appeared so menacing to Brock that he cut short his leave and, without waiting for the regular packet, sailed for Quebec on a little Guernsey ship that had been fitted out as a privateer.

When Brock arrived in Canada for the second time, he was appointed temporary commander-in-chief of all the armed forces. Although he was to hold this appointment only until some more senior officer came out from England to replace him, Brock seized the opportunity of preparing for the war he feared was coming. He soon set about making the changes he felt necessary.

As always, his first concern was with the defence of Upper and Lower Canada against an American invasion. Since there were so few British troops in Canada it was considered impossible to protect the entire country against an American attack. The plan was for Quebec to be held strongly but for the garrisons elsewhere to make a fighting retirement back to the old Citadel. Because of the long, hard Canadian winter, the Americans would not be able to besiege Quebec after the first frosts came but would have to retreat to their bases in the United States. Then, in the spring, when the St. Lawrence River was again open to navigation, Britain would send reinforcements to Canada and the counter-attack would begin. The chances were that the second season of campaigning would be very different from the first.

The success of this plan, of course, depended upon the ability of the British to hold Quebec against attack. The ancient fortress was built in a strong natural position but it had not been put to the test of battle for thirty years. The last time the guns of Quebec had been fired in anger was when American troops had assaulted the Citadel in a driving snow-storm on New Year's Eve of 1776. The Americans had been driven back in disorder, but since then the fortifications had been allowed to fall into disrepair.

Brock discovered that the west wall, in particular, needed strengthening, for it was so old and decayed that it would not be able to withstand a sustained fire. He estimated that he would need 600 to 1,000 men every day for six weeks or two months to make the repairs. The garrison was too small to provide such a labour force, and the civilian government of the province was unwilling to act.

Far from being discouraged by this lack of co-operation, Brock went ahead with the repair of the fortifications as best he could. Besides strengthening the walls, he created clear fields of fire around the ramparts, obtained a new parade-ground on which his soldiers could drill, and mounted a battery of eight thirty-six-pounder guns above

the centre of the Citadel, so that they could fire down upon the opposite heights at Levis. The townspeople of Quebec called this gun-site "Brock's Battery", but when a new Governor-in-Chief, Sir James Craig, arrived in October 1807, he changed the title to "The King's Battery". Brock good-naturedly wrote to his brothers that this change of name was "the greatest compliment, I conceive, that [Sir James] could pay to my judgement".

Brock's days, and often his nights as well, were taken up with a host of administrative details. He worked hard and insisted that those under him work hard too, for he had the feeling that he was racing against time, that the peace with the United States might be broken at any moment.

He soon found that more than the fortifications of

Quebec had been neglected. The Commissary-General, whose duty it was to supply the army, had not had a proper audit of some of his accounts since 1788, and, when Brock insisted that this be done at once, the Commissary-General protested that no one in Canada had the authority to make him produce his books. Brock was not the man to tolerate this sort of nonsense. He replied that he had been given the command and that he intended to exercise it "with promptitude and decision". The audit took place and – just as Brock had suspected – large sums could not be accounted for. The Commissary-General was dismissed in disgrace.

Always careful of the welfare of his men, Brock exerted himself to have a new military hospital built at Quebec, and was careful to see that each soldier received the full pay and allowances that were his due. He hoped to raise some units of Canadian militia to help the British regulars in the event of war, but there was much opposition to this plan. Sir James Craig, badly advised by his secretary, Ryland, who hated the French Canadians, was afraid to place arms in the hands of the habitants, and in Upper Canada the population was too sparse – and in some districts too sympathetic with the Americans – for any sizeable number of militia to be raised. One such corps, however, was later formed among the Canadians of Scottish descent around Glengarry. As time went on and the danger of war increased, other Canadian militia units were raised. They fought bravely once war had begun.

Perhaps more important than any of these tasks was Brock's reorganization of the military shipping on the

Great Lakes. Brock ordered that forty-one boats for the transport of troops be kept in constant repair at Quebec, Three Rivers, Montreal, St. Johns, Kingston, Fort George, York, and Amherstburg. These precautions of Brock's meant that, when war did break out in 1812, British troops were never prevented from moving because of a shortage of shipping.

Early in 1808 Brock was posted to command the garrison in Montreal, an appointment he held until September when he returned to Quebec. While in Montreal he was promoted to brigadier-general.

Although Quebec and Montreal were already notice-
ably different, both cities had a gay social life. Quebec
was the seat of the government and the headquarters of
the Commander-in-Chief. British naval vessels put in
there regularly, and distinguished visitors often arrived.
There were balls for the garrison, picnics in the woods,
country trips, races, and many dinner parties. Brock entered into all this with his usual zest, later writing to his
sister-in-law: "I contributed my share to the general mirth
in a grand dinner given to Mrs. Gore [the wife of the
Lieutenant-Governor of Upper Canada] at which Sir J.

Craig was present, and a ball to a vast assemblage of all descriptions."

Montreal, on the other hand, was the headquarters of the rich merchants of the North West Company, the "Lords of the North", who ran a vast fur-trading empire extending over the entire north-west of the continent. When he was stationed in Montreal, Brock frequently dined with these men and listened to their strange tales of the "great lone land" beyond the last outposts of civilization.

Brock was never too busy, however, to do kindnesses for those about him. Ex-officers or soldiers who asked his help in finding employment were seldom disappointed, and he was as generous in praising those who did good work as he was strict with the careless and the lazy. When a former officer died, leaving his widow and children poorly provided for, Brock obtained a commission as ensign for the oldest boy and arranged for the widow and other children to be given free lodging and rations. Not long afterwards he obtained free rations for a penniless old soldier of the 8th Foot.

On this occasion Sir James Craig had one of his staff officers write to Brock: "I am to remind you of the danger of establishing a precedent of this nature, and to request, in the general's name, that you will refrain as much as possible from indulging the natural benevolence of your disposition in this way, as he has hitherto resisted all applications of this sort."

This mild reproof did not deter Brock from helping the less fortunate whenever he could. There were people in every part of Upper and Lower Canada who knew his good nature and thought of him with love and gratitude.

He was, of course, especially fond of his own family and corresponded with them regularly. In the summer of 1810 in a letter to his sister-in-law, he asked after his two nieces and added: "If I am able in the fall to procure handsome skins for muffs worth their acceptance, I shall send some to the dear little girls." And on another occasion he wrote his brother Irving, thanking him for making some purchases for him in England, and saying: "The different articles arrived in the very best order, with the exception of the cocked hat which has not been received – a most distressing circumstance, as, from the enormity of my head, I find the utmost difficulty in getting a substitute in this country."

Although Brock enjoyed himself in Montreal and Quebec and although he worked hard to improve Canada's defences, he wanted very badly to return to England in order to get into action. His brother Savery had fought with Sir John Moore in Spain in 1808, when the British had been forced out after the Battle of Corunna. Now a new British army, commanded by Lord Wellington, was slowly reconquering Spain and Portugal from Napoleon's troops. Brock naturally believed that it was in the Peninsula that glory was to be won and he knew that if he could only get to England he could obtain command of a brigade in Wellington's army. Sir James Craig, however, had too high an opinion of Brock's military ability to let him go, and all his applications for leave were kindly but definitely rejected.

4. Upper Canada on the Eve of War

In the late summer of 1810 Brock was sent to command the military forces in Upper Canada. He did not much relish the change, for he had grown used to Quebec and had made himself comfortable there. Also, he was afraid that after he had moved all his belongings to York at great expense he might be recalled to Lower Canada by Sir James Craig.

"But I must submit to all this without repining," he wrote in a letter home, "and since I cannot get to Europe I care little where I am placed."

Still, he left the old, grey-stone town reluctantly, almost as though he sensed he would never see it again.

"I have the most beautiful garden imaginable," he told his sister-in-law, "with an abundance of melons and other good things, all of which I must now desert."

Brock was too friendly a man and too full of life to find even the little backwoods capital of York dull for long. He worked hard, and for relaxation he fished the wilderness streams. When autumn came, he shot wild pigeons in the woods. As was natural for him, he entered fully into the social life of the provincial capital. His old friends in the upper province were delighted to see him again, and he quickly made new ones.

He was a frequent visitor at Tordarroch, the large log mansion of the Adjutant-General of Militia, Aeneas Shaw. Although there are no written records to support it, tradition has it that during his visits there he fell in love with Susan Shaw, one of the General's daughters, and that they would have married had the outbreak of war not interrupted their plans.

By now the threat of invasion hung all along the frontier, like thunderheads piling up on the horizon. Sooner or later the storm was bound to break. Everyone knew it, from Isaac Brock to the youngest drummer boy. The farmers in the scattered border settlements knew it and waited for the Americans to come – fearful or hopeful, depending on whether they were Loyalists or new homesteaders from the United States. Every soldier on sentry duty at the lonely outpost forts knew it and was nervously alert for the attack that might come suddenly in the night.

Relations between Britain and the United States had grown steadily worse. Britain was now at war with France, and Napoleon had passed a series of laws, the "Berlin Decrees", which closed the ports of Europe to British vessels. Britain retaliated by forbidding any neutral ship to enter a port under French control unless it had first been inspected in England. Many American ships that tried to run the British blockade were seized by the Royal Navy.

Because British sailors who deserted from the navy often went to sea again on American ships, the British insisted that they had the right to stop American vessels on the high seas and search them for deserters. These searches were sometimes carried out in an arrogant manner. In 1807, for instance, war had almost been declared because the British man-of-war *Leopard* had fired a broadside into the American frigate *Chesapeake*, during such a search, and killed some American sailors. Occasionally, by mistake, native-born American citizens were forced into service with the Royal Navy.

These occasional violent encounters in the Atlantic, provocative as they were, would by themselves probably not have led the United States to declare war on Britain. A more serious cause of quarrel was the trouble American settlers west of the Ohio River were having with the Indians, who were Britain's allies. As the Americans pushed farther and farther west, the Indians were forced to abandon their hunting-grounds and retreat before the advance of civilization. Fearing that they would eventually lose their whole country to the white man, the Indians fought back, raiding and burning isolated settlements and killing the settlers.

Neither side showed much mercy in this conflict. The Indians commonly massacred and scalped all the whites who fell into their hands, including the women and children, often after torturing them. The settlers, in turn, looked upon the Indians as savages who were scarcely human.

The British got along well with the Indians. Many of the tribes had fought beside the British in the American Revolutionary War, and, since there were no British colonists moving out to occupy the West, there was little cause for conflict. British fur traders were active west of the Ohio River, however, and the American settlers claimed, with some truth, that they were supplying the Indians with muskets, ammunition, and liquor. Nothing would persuade the homesteaders that the British government was not deliberately stirring up the Indians to attack American outposts.

In fact, Sir James Craig issued strict orders that the Indians were to be discouraged from harrying the Americans, and when Brock came to Upper Canada he did his best to enforce this policy. Britain did not want a war with the United States while she was fighting Napoleon, yet Brock knew that without the assistance of the Indians he could not defend Upper Canada from an American invasion.

Every year hundreds of braves gathered at Amherstburg to trade and to receive blankets, muskets, gunpowder, bar lead, bullet moulds, and other supplies, as gifts from the government. Brock complained that he had no control over the Indian Department whose superintendent, Matthew Elliott, continued to supply the savages with "a liberal quantity of military stores". Consequently, Brock could not entirely restrain his Indian allies from resisting the American settlement of the West, although this brought nearer the war he wished to avoid.

In the spring of 1811, Sir James Craig's health, which had never been good, finally broke down and he decided to return to England, knowing he might die there. Before he left he sent word to Brock, apologizing again for being unable to agree to his requests for leave. Craig's reasons

were the same as before – war might break out with the
United States at any moment. Only that May another
ugly incident had occurred at sea, when the United States
frigate *President* had attacked and badly damaged the

British sloop *Little Belt*. In the circumstances, Brock simply could not be spared.

Sir James was genuinely sorry to hold his best officer in Canada against his will, and, as a mark of affection, he asked Brock to accept his favourite horse, Alfred, a high-bred ten-year-old. Despite Alfred's age, he was an excellent mount, and Sir James knew that in Brock his old favourite would find a kind and careful master. When Alfred was brought to York that summer Brock instantly took to the big grey horse, perhaps because he had a sympathy with anything that was both gentle and spirited. With the outbreak of war the following year Alfred served as Brock's charger.

That June Brock was promoted to major-general on the staff of North America. The new Governor-in-Chief and Captain-General of the Forces, Sir George Prevost, arrived in September. He was a small man of forty-six, with charming manners and a friendly, placid air. Doubtless he would have been an excellent governor in times of peace, for he was a wise and understanding administrator, but he was to prove a timid and uncertain leader in time of war. Probably he and Brock never met, for shortly after Prevost's arrival Brock was appointed temporary president and administrator of Upper Canada while Lieutenant-Governor Gore was on leave of absence in England.

On the eve of war, General Brock thus found himself in charge of both the civilian and military branches of the government of Upper Canada. He had reached this high office at the early age of forty-two, and had done so, moreover, entirely by his own character and ability. Modest as he was, he must have felt a certain just pride in his achievement.

October 6 was Brock's forty-second birthday, and the General was in high spirits. He had heard that a government schooner was to put into York harbour that morning with mail from England. Private Dobson was at the dock almost before the ship tied up, for he knew how eager the General always was for word from his family. Half an hour later Dobson knocked on Brock's office door, entered, and placed a bundle of newspapers on the desk.

"Sorry, sir. No letters this time. But there'll be another mail in a week or two."

The General's face fell. He had not heard from England for several months and had thought it certain he would get a long letter from Irving and probably one of Savery's cheerful notes as well. A flicker of apprehension crossed his mind, but he dismissed it. If any of his family were ill, the others would certainly have written to tell him. Rather wryly he turned to the newspapers, hoping that he would at least learn something of old army friends who were fighting with Lord Wellington in Spain.

The papers were those of the previous summer, and as Brock looked them over he saw that times were none too good in England. More bankruptcies had occurred in 1811 than in any previous year in Britain's history. All over the country warehouses were filled with goods that could not be sold, while the wharfs and quays of the ports were deserted.

That summer some London merchants had made a desperate effort to revive their Baltic trade. They had loaded a number of ships, paid heavy premiums to insure them through Lloyd's, and sent them to sea, bound for Russia, Sweden, and Prussia. Almost all of this merchant armada was lost – some ships were sunk in a storm, some were captured off the European coast by privateers, and most of the remainder were seized in port and confiscated by Napoleon's orders. The merchants and bankers who had backed the venture or insured the ships were ruined. A list of the bankruptcies followed, and, as Brock glanced over it, one name suddenly stood out on the page: his brother William's banking-house and trading company had been declared insolvent the previous June.

The General sat quite still at his desk, his brown face pale beneath its tan. This meant financial ruin for most of his family, and William, his eldest brother, who had always been more like a father to him, might never recover from the loss and humiliation. All Brock's thoughts were for William and his wife Sally and of how he could help them.

The next day, when he had had time to arrange his thoughts, he wrote to Savery, offering what assistance he could give: "I write merely to say, for really my poor head will not allow me to say more, that tomorrow I enter into the official duties of president of this province. The salary attached to the situation is £1,000, the whole of which, I trust, I shall be able to save, and after a year or two even more. . . . Yesterday was the first truly gloomy birthday I have ever passed."

There was still worse to come. On October 30 Brock at last received a letter from one of his family – it had been written by Irving on August 3 – and thus learned the full extent of the disaster. Years before, William had given him £3,000 for the purchase of his commissions. This had been a private transaction, and William, who had no children of his own, had never intended that the money should be repaid, but by mistake the sum had been entered as a loan on the books of the bank. Now General Brock was to be sued by William's creditors for the whole amount, which was quite above his power to repay unless he sold his commission. It looked as though his brilliant military career was to be brought to a sudden end.

This was certainly bad enough, but what hurt him even more was that the failure of the banking house had led to a quarrel between William and Irving, who had been in the business together. To Isaac Brock, who was so deeply fond of all his brothers, this last news was harder to bear than any other. He immediately wrote to Irving:

I have at length heard from you. Your letter of the 3rd August was only received this day. To what a state of misery are we fallen – poverty I was prepared to bear – but, oh! Irving, if you love me, do not by any action or word add to the sorrows of poor, unfortunate William. Remember his kindness to me – what pleasure he always found in doing me service. Hang the world, it is not worth a thought – be generous and find silent comfort in being so. Oh! my dear boy, forget the past, and let us all unite in soothing the griefs of one of the best hearts that Heaven ever formed. I can well conceive that the causes of his ruin were excited by too ardent a wish to place us all in affluence – his wealth we were sure to divide – why refuse him consolation? – it is all, alas! I can offer. . . . I sleep little, but am constrained to assume a smiling face during the day: my thoughts are fixed upon you all. . . . You know the position to which I am lately raised. It will enable me to give up the whole of my salary, £1,000 yearly, and I shall enclose a power of attorney to enable you to receive it – do with it what justice demands – pay as fast as you receive, unless indeed want among any of you calls for aid; in that case make use of the money, and let the worst come. I leave everything to your sober discretion.

It was fortunate for Brock that he was so busy, for his work enabled him to forget his private troubles. By now he was certain that President Madison would be forced to declare war on Britain. A group of some thirty tumultuous young Congressmen from the West and South, known as the "War Hawks", were determined to drive Britain completely out of North America.

The leader of the War Hawks was the fiery Henry Clay of Kentucky, the Speaker of the House of Representatives. He and his followers, who had been too young to fight in the American Revolutionary War, were anxious to rival the deeds of their fathers. And what better time to declare war than when almost all of Britain's ships and soldiers were busy fighting the French? The War Hawks frankly said that they intended to invade and annex Canada.

"I am not for stopping at Quebec or anywhere else," Clay declared publicly. "I would take the entire continent." And on another occasion he said: "The conquest of Canada is in our power . . . the militia of Kentucky are alone competent to place Montreal and Upper Canada at your feet."

Isaac Brock thought differently.

He did not underestimate the difficulties. The United States had a population more than twenty times as large as that of both Canadian provinces combined and was far wealthier and better developed. Even worse, every pound of gunpowder and shot, every musket and cannon, and most of the military supplies needed by British troops in Upper Canada had to come from across the Atlantic and be brought forward by the long water route of the St. Lawrence River and the Great Lakes. If the Americans cut this supply line, all the territory west of the point of attack would have to be abandoned. In contrast, the invading armies could be supplied as far as the Canadian border by a reasonably good road system.

In January, 1812, President Madison authorized the regular army of the United States to be increased to 35,000, and later ordered 10,000 militiamen to be called up, in addition to 50,000 short-term volunteers. To meet this threat there were, in the whole of the Canadas, only some 5,000 British soldiers, a few hundred Canadian militia, and Britain's Indian allies. To most people the only possible plan for the defence of Canada seemed to be the old one of retreating to the Citadel of Quebec and abandoning all the rest of the country to the invaders until help could arrive from overseas.

Brock, however, hated to do this. He was reluctant to retreat without a fight, and he knew that both the Canadians and the Indians would feel forsaken and betrayed if he did. To abandon Upper Canada would lose him the help of the militia and his Indian allies. Moreover, he had thought deeply about the military situation and believed he could detect certain weaknesses in the American position. Accordingly he made a plan.

The plan was typical of Brock – bold almost to the point of rashness but nevertheless based on sound common sense.

The enemy outnumbered him? He could expect little help from Britain during the first year of the war? It was impossible to defend the 1,200-mile frontier with the forces he had available? Very well then, he would attack.

He wrote a long dispatch to the new Governor-in-Chief, outlining his ideas. Before the Americans could invade, they would have to take time to organize and assemble their armies. Brock proposed to strike quickly during this period, upsetting the enemy's plans and discouraging the American population.

The British force in Canada was small, but it consisted of well-trained, disciplined regulars and would be supported by some militia and Indians. It could attack on the western frontier, capturing both Fort Detroit and the fort on Michilimackinac Island at the upper end of Lake Huron. These posts were weakly garrisoned – Brock estimated that neither of them had more than seventy defenders, but he guessed that Detroit would be reinforced as soon as war was declared. If these forts fell to a sudden surprise attack, the Indians would come in whole-heartedly on the British side and the Canadians would be convinced that the government did not intend to desert them.

The essence of this plan was speed, surprise, and boldness. The prudent Sir George Prevost must have shuddered when he read it. He still hoped that, after all, war might never be declared. Therefore he did not forbid Brock to carry out his plan but merely warned him to do nothing that might provoke the Americans.

In January of 1812, word arrived from England that General Brock, if he wished, could leave Canada and take a command in Spain. This was exactly what he had dreamed of for so long, but now, when it was finally possible, his sense of duty would not allow him to go.

So he remained in Upper Canada, building up stores of ammunition and equipment, raising new militia units, strengthening the frontier forts, inspecting his troops, and encouraging the civilian population to resist. He made large purchases of flour and Indian corn in the United States, so that "our own stocks may remain un-diminished". He again pressed his plan of campaign on Sir George Prevost, warning him "that unless Detroit and Michilimackinac be both in our possession immediately at the commencement of hostilities, not only the district of Amherstburg but most probably the whole country as far as Kingston, must be evacuated". He was disappointed when the Legislature of Upper Canada refused to pass all the emergency bills he considered necessary, but neither this setback nor his serious shortages of men and supplies discouraged him.

During these last months of peace he worked tirelessly, often for sixteen hours and more a day. He seemed to be always on the move – to Fort George, to Amherstburg, to Queenston, to the Six Nations Indians on the Grand River. His huge, soldierly figure on his big grey charger, Alfred, was a familiar sight along the frontier, and wherever he went his presence lifted the spirits of his soldiers.

A thousand things had to be done before summer came – and with summer the Americans.

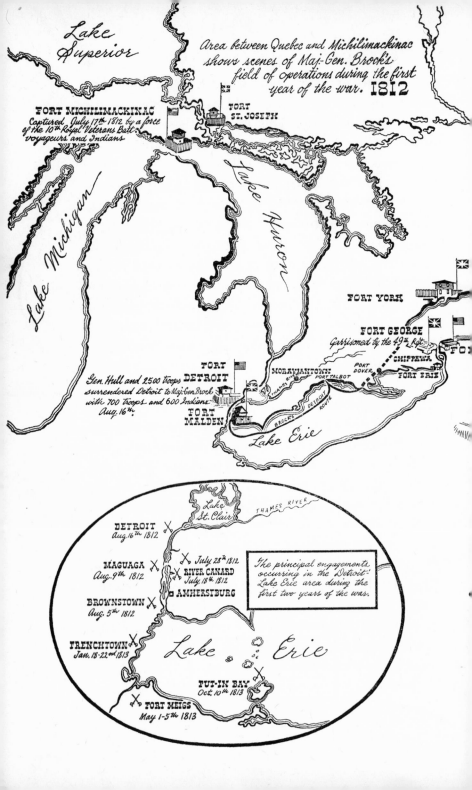

Lake Superior

Area between Quebec and Michilimackinac shows scenes of Maj.-Gen. Brock's field of operations during the first year of the war. 1812

FORT MICHILIMACKINAC
Captured July 17th 1812 by a force of the 10th Royal Veterans Batt. voyageurs and Indians

FORT ST. JOSEPH

Lake Michigan

Lake Huron

FORT YORK

FORT GEORGE
Garrisoned by the 49th Rgt.

PORT DOVER

CHIPPAWA

FORT ERIE

Gen. Hull and 2500 troops surrendered Detroit to Maj.-Gen. Brock with 700 troops and 600 Indians Aug. 16th.

FORT DETROIT

MORAVIANTOWN
PORT TALBOT
THAMES RIVER
DETROIT ROUTE
BAGLEY'S

FORT MALDEN

Lake Erie

DETROIT
Aug. 16th 1812

Lake St. Clair

THAMES RIVER

MAGUAGA
Aug. 9th 1812

July 25th 1812
RIVER CANARD
July 18th 1812
AMHERSTBURG

The principal engagements occuring in the Detroit-Lake Erie area during the first two years of the war.

BROWNSTOWN
Aug. 5th 1812

FRENCHTOWN
Jan. 18-22nd 1813

Lake Erie

PUT-IN BAY
Oct. 10th 1813

FORT MEIGS
May 1-5th 1813

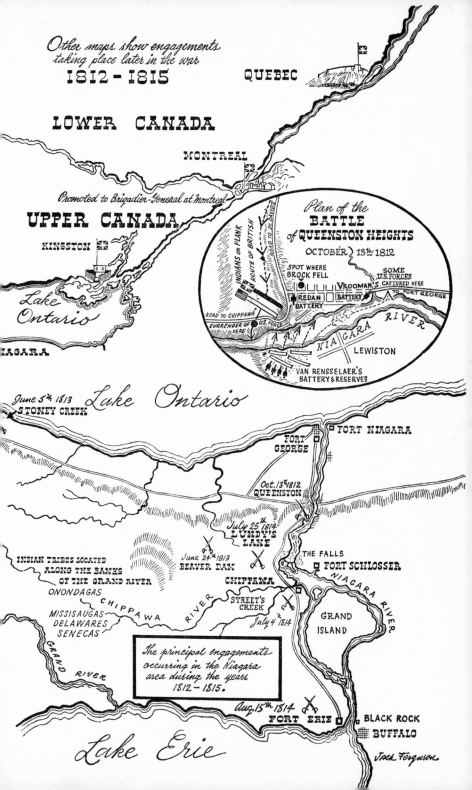

Other maps show engagements taking place later in the war
1812 - 1815

QUEBEC

LOWER CANADA

MONTREAL

Promoted to Brigadier-General at Montreal

UPPER CANADA

KINGSTON

Lake Ontario

NIAGARA

Plan of the
BATTLE
of QUEENSTON HEIGHTS
OCTOBER 13th 1812

INDIANS on FLANK
ROUTE OF BRITISH
ROAD TO CHIPPAWA
SURRENDER OF U.S. FORCE
HERE

SPOT WHERE
BROCK FELL

SOME
U.S. FORCES
CAPTURED HERE

VROOMAN'S

REDAN
BATTERY

BATTERY

TO FORT GEORGE

NIAGARA RIVER

LEWISTON

VAN RENSSELAER'S
BATTERY & RESERVES

June 5th 1813
STONEY CREEK

Lake Ontario

FORT NIAGARA

FORT
GEORGE

Oct. 13th 1812
QUEENSTON

July 25th 1814
LUNDY'S LANE

THE FALLS

FORT SCHLOSSER

June 24th 1813
BEAVER DAM

INDIAN TRIBES LOCATED
ALONG THE BANKS
OF THE GRAND RIVER
ONONDAGAS

MISSISAUGAS
DELAWARES
SENECAS

CHIPPAWA

CHIPPAWA   RIVER

STREET'S
CREEK

July 4th 1814

GRAND
ISLAND

NIAGARA RIVER

GRAND   RIVER

The principal engagements
occurring in the Niagara
area during the years
1812 - 1815.

Aug. 15th 1814

FORT ERIE

BLACK ROCK

BUFFALO

Lake Erie

Jack Ferguson

5. The Outbreak of War

THOMAS Clark of Queenston was the local agent for the John Jacob Astor fur-trading company of New York, but he was also a patriotic Canadian. So when the company messenger came pounding on his door in the cool dawn of June 25, Clark already knew what he had to do. He had been half expecting such a message.

He came out to his doorstep, rubbing the sleep from his eyes, and tore open the envelope the messenger thrust at him. It was a special express from Washington. As he had anticipated, it contained word that the United States Congress and Senate had voted for war against Britain. The company had made haste to inform him of this because it was anxious for its agents to halt the dispatch of furs from its depots in the North-west.

Clark thanked the messenger and hurried back to his bedroom to dress. Word of this must be sent to General Brock at once.

Brock was in his office at York when Clark's news reached him that same afternoon. The General read the message carefully, his face sober and thoughtful. The vote for war had been taken on the 18th – just a week ago. The fur company's messenger must have ridden hard to reach

Queenston so quickly. The General called in his brigade-major, Thomas Evans, and began to issue his orders.

It was fortunate that Brock did not wait for official confirmation from Sir George Prevost, because the Governor-in-Chief himself was not notified until July 7, and Brock did not receive official word for a full five weeks. As it was, Brock learned of the outbreak of war before some American commanders, and he made good use of the time granted him.

The British government was not informed of the declaration of war until July 30. By then the objectionable orders in council allowing the Royal Navy to seize and search American ships had already been repealed, and the British cabinet believed that, when the United States learned of this, peace would speedily be restored. Consequently, Britain made little effort to reinforce Canada in 1812.

In fact, President Madison had signed the declaration of war on the same day that Congress had taken its final vote. The War Hawks were to have the conflict for which they had been clamouring, but many Americans bitterly disagreed with them. Congress had voted only 79 to 49 for war; in the Senate the vote had been even closer – 19 to 13. In general, the southern and western states were eager to fight, while the northern and eastern states wanted peace. In Boston the feeling against "Mr. Madison's War" was so strong that the flags were flown at half-mast, and some New Englanders even spoke of breaking away from the Union.

Sir George Prevost, who had been born in the United States and had many friends there, hated the idea of war and was anxious to do nothing that would unite the Americans. He seemed to hope even now that everything could still be arranged without fighting. Three weeks after the declaration of war he was still urging Brock not to attack, and just five days before an American army invaded Canada he was assuring him that the United States was too divided to be any serious danger.

General Brock did not share Sir George Prevost's opinion. Within half an hour of the arrival of Thomas Clark's letter, the military headquarters in York was crackling with activity. Young officers hurriedly saddled their horses and galloped off in the late afternoon sunlight to carry word to British garrisons along the frontier. In York Harbour, ships hoisted sail and put out from land on the same mission. Before darkness fell, two companies of the 41st Regiment had filed aboard a schooner and been sent to reinforce Fort George. Eight hundred Canadians were called out on active service with the newly-formed flank companies and issued with what military stores were available.

When these measures had been taken, General Brock, in his capacity as President of Upper Canada, called his Council together. They gathered at the General's headquarters that night, a group of earnest, rather frightened men, who sat around the long table in the lamplight and listened apprehensively to what Brock had to say. The curtains by the open window stirred in the warm air, and in the dark garden outside a sentry stamped and banged his musket as he turned and ordered arms at the end of his beat.

Brock's voice was quiet and matter-of-fact; it soothed and steadied his listeners, making them forget their fears. Soon they were leaning forward in their chairs, sensibly discussing what had to be done. At Brock's suggestion they decided to hold a special session of the Legislature as soon as possible, and then, comforted, they left. Brock accompanied them to the door and bade them good-night with his usual cheerful friendliness.

The Council members returned to their homes through the dark streets of York, but for General Brock the long day was not yet over. Taking with him his brigade-major, Evans, his aide-de-camp, Captain John Glegg, and eleven men, he went down to the harbour and requisitioned a small boat. In this he set out for Fort George to assume command of the vital Niagara frontier in person.

Apparently he had no great confidence in the local commander at Fort George. This was not surprising, for, although that commander was now a major-general, he was still the same Roger Sheaffe who as junior lieutenant-colonel of the 49th had been better at provoking his men to mutiny than at dealing with a rebellion after it had broken out.

Now for the second time Brock was making the thirty-mile trip across the open lake in a *bateau,* a journey few cared to undertake even in daylight. He gave no thought to the possible dangers. Having done all that he could, his mind was at rest. He dozed comfortably in the stern sheets as the boat thrust its way through the dark water towards Fort George. He needed to snatch a little sleep when he could, for he had no idea when he would get the chance again.

Certainly Brock had little rest in the next few days. When he reached Fort George he found that several American gentlemen, including some officers from Fort Niagara, were Sheaffe's guests. Brock politely informed them that war had been declared, insisted that they stay for lunch, then sent them back across the river with Captain Glegg under a flag of truce. That afternoon Brock borrowed a horse and set out to inspect the thirty-five-mile stretch of frontier beween Fort George and Fort Erie. He strengthened the guards along the river and saw to it that the men were as well provided for as the equipment at hand permitted. He studied reports on the American forces massing opposite him. And, among other appointments, he made his old friend Robert Nichol, the little Scots storekeeper of Niagara, Quartermaster-General of Militia with the rank of lieutenant-colonel. This was a shrewd move, for in the coming campaign Nichol was to prove himself an excellent soldier, but at the time a number of officers were offended at Nichol's appointment. They could see only that he was a vain, uneducated man, and could not discern, as Brock did, his gifts of spirit and intelligence.

One of General Brock's first acts at Fort George was to write Captain Charles Roberts, who was in command at Fort Joseph, ordering him to capture the American post at Michilimackinac, some fifty miles away. Just as Brock had foreseen, the American preparations for annexing Canada were going slowly. The Americans had deluded themselves into thinking that the conquest of Canada would be "a mere matter of marching" and so their war plan called for three widely separated invasions. Their wisest course would have been to concentrate against Montreal, because its capture would have cut off all of Upper Canada from supplies and reinforcements. Instead, they decided to invade with one army at Detroit, another along the Niagara frontier, and a third at Lake Champlain. None of these armies expected to meet much real opposition; the Americans thought the Canadians would greet them as liberators.

General William Hull, a fifty-nine-year-old lawyer who was Governor of Michigan, was to command the North West Army at Detroit; General Stephen Van Rensselaer, a wealthy politician from New York, was to command the Central Army along the Niagara River; and General Henry Dearborn, a sixty-one-year-old veteran of the American Revolutionary War, who was popularly known as "Granny" and who was so fat that he had to travel in a specially-built carriage, was nominal commander-in-chief and in charge of the Northern Army, which would assemble at Lake Champlain.

Long before war was declared, the Americans had been enrolling volunteers, organizing regiments, and electing their officers. On June 1, General Hull's army, which had mustered at Dayton, Ohio, began its march. Its first aim was to reinforce Detroit; from there it would cross into Canada to roll up General Brock's forces from the west. Hull's army, over 2,200 strong, ultimately consisted of one regular regiment, the 4th U.S. Infantry, three regiments of Ohio Volunteers, and some Michigan militia. Only the regulars had uniforms; the volunteers had been hastily outfitted with homespun hunting shirts, trousers, wide leather belts, and low-crowned felt hats. The men were badly disciplined, believing, not unreasonably, that they knew as much about war as their officers, but the Ohio Volunteers, especially, were tough and hardy, and most of them were first-class rifle shots. Since the commanding officers of the three Volunteer regiments held the militia rank of full colonel, they were jealously distrustful of the more experienced lieutenant-colonel who commanded the 4th Regiment of regulars.

Hull himself was not an inspiring commander. He was a big, stout, red-faced man who was obsessed with the fear that he would sometime be ambushed by Indians. His headquarters had rather the appearance of being a family affair, for he took his son and his son-in-law along with him as his aides-de-camp.

To reach Detroit, Hull had to make a long march through difficult Indian country, and almost from the first things began to go wrong. At Urbana on June 15 some of his Ohio Volunteers mutinied because they had not been paid, and he had to call in the regulars to make them continue the march. Although the Americans did not know it, Indian scouts friendly to the British watched every move of Hull's army as it plodded through the swampy wilderness towards Detroit.

Worse than any of this was the United States government's failure to tell Hull of the outbreak of war until July 2, a full week after Brock knew of it. On July 1 Hull had reached the mouth of the Miami River on Lake Erie, and there, believing that his country was still at peace, he had hired the schooner *Cayahoga* to carry his heavy baggage, musical instruments, and medical stores to Detroit. The sick and some regimental musicians were also placed aboard the *Cayahoga* and, as an afterthought, the General's son stowed away a chest containing Hull's official correspondence and the muster-rolls of the army. General Hull with the army continued by land to Detroit. Unfortunately for him, Brock had been prompter than the American government in letting his subordinates know of the declaration of war. The next morning, when the *Cayahoga* was sailing unconcernedly up the Detroit River past

Amherstburg, the British brig *General Hunter* ordered her to heave to and surrender.

A small boarding party swarmed over the *Cayahoga*'s side, declared the American soldiers to be prisoners of war, ran up the Union Jack to the mast-head, and then assembled the captured regimental musicians on the after-

deck and had them play "God Save the King". The captured correspondence and muster-rolls were sent to Brock at Fort George. For quite some time thereafter Brock knew more about the North West Army than Hull himself.

On July 6 Hull finally entered Detroit. He was relieved that the long march was over, and for the next four days rested his army, preparatory to crossing to the Canadian side of the Detroit River and capturing the village of Sandwich. The invasion was scheduled for the night of the 10th; boats were gathered, the troops were alerted, and final orders were issued. The attack was to take place at dawn.

An hour or two before daylight on July 10 the sleeping Americans were suddenly aroused by a musket-shot and a sentry's voice crying: "Indians! We're being attacked by Indians!"

More shots followed as other nervous sentries blazed away at every patch of shadow around the perimeter of the fort. Soldiers struggled up from sleep and rushed here and there in the darkness, shouting and firing off their muskets indiscriminately. At least one officer was seriously wounded, battalions became hopelessly mixed up, and some men mislaid their equipment. When dawn came, it was obvious that all idea of crossing the river that day would have to be abandoned. With the morning too, Hull discovered that the whole thing had been a false alarm and that no hostile Indians had been within miles of Fort Detroit.

At dawn on the 12th the North West Army finally

crossed the river and entered Canada. It met no resistance, for the small British force opposite had withdrawn to Amherstburg. General Hull issued a proclamation in which he said:

Inhabitants of Canada!
... The army under my command has invaded your country and the standard of union now waves over the territory of Canada. .... I come prepared for every contingency. I have a force which will look down all opposition, and that force is but the vanguard of a much greater. .... If the barbarous and savage policy of Great Britain be pursued, and the savages let loose to murder our citizens, and butcher our women and children, this war will be a war of extermination. The first stroke of the tomahawk, the first attempt with the scalping knife, will be the signal of one indiscriminate scene of desolation. No white man, found fighting by the side of an Indian, will be taken prisoner – instant destruction will be his lot. .... The United States offer you peace, liberty, and security. Your choice lies between these and war, slavery and destruction. Choose, then, but choose wisely. ....

After this notice had been posted up in Sandwich, Hull's army settled down to fortify its camp.

Far away from Detroit, Captain Roberts at Fort Joseph was reading a letter General Brock had written him on June 28, telling him again that he could attack Michilimackinac if he thought he could capture it. Roberts, who although in poor health was a keen and aggressive officer, knew how Brock felt about the capture of Michilimackinac and was anxious to secure his general's good opinion.

Probably, indeed, Brock had sent him to Fort Joseph with this very possibility in mind, for Brock knew his officers and what each could do. It was true that Sir George Prevost had written Roberts on June 25, ordering him to act only on the defensive "with the greatest vigilance and Caution" and to be ready "in Case of Necessity [for] the ultimate retreat of your Party", but Brock's order bore the more recent date. Roberts decided to act at once before he received another command from the Governor-in-Chief to do nothing.

Fort Michilimackinac, fifty miles south-west of Fort Joseph, stood on a high limestone cliff at the south-eastern

PROCLAMATION
INHABITANTS *of* CANADA

end of the little island that guarded the entrance to Lake Michigan. The sturdy log fort, armed with nine-pounder guns, was garrisoned by sixty-one American soldiers under Lieutenant Porter Hanks. Captain Roberts had forty-six regulars of the 10th Royal Veterans Battalion and he had mustered about 180 French-Canadian *voyageurs* of the North West Company under Toussaint Pothier, a Hudson's Bay Company agent. In addition, a number of Indians agreed to accompany the little expedition.

On July 16, Roberts loaded his soldiers and *voyageurs* on board the North West Company's schooner *Caledonia* and set off for Michilimackinac. The Indians, who thought nothing of making such a trip in calm weather, came along in their big war canoes.

Roberts's force reached the island after midnight. Not a light shone out from the fort or the little village beside it as the *Caledonia* tacked about to circle Michilimackinac to the north. There, on a deserted stretch of beach where the black spruce forest came down almost to the shoreline, the attackers crept silently ashore at three o'clock in the morning. A six-pounder gun was slung overside from the *Caledonia*'s main deck and dragged ashore. Then two dozen *voyageurs*, sweating at the drag-ropes and straining against the wheels, manhandled it along dark forest paths to the top of a steep hill overlooking the fort.

By daybreak everything was ready. When Lieutenant Hanks looked out from his fort to see Roberts's men and their gun at his rear, he decided not to fight it out. After a brief parley, the American flag came fluttering down and the white flag of surrender broke out over Michilimackinac.

This daring little raid captured sixty-two American officers and men, seven cannon, and a well-provisioned fort, but its results were far greater than that. Exactly as Brock had predicted, as soon as the Indians heard of the capture of Michilimackinac they were convinced that the British intended to fight for Upper Canada. In the next few weeks they flocked in their hundreds to Amherstburg to join in the battle against their old enemies, the Americans.

The war was now a month old. Brock had drawn first blood, and one of the two forts whose capture he considered absolutely necessary had already fallen.

Next it would be the turn of Fort Detroit.

6. Brock Meets Tecumseh

GENERAL Brock did not hear of Hull's invasion until July 20, when he received a dispatch from Lieutenant-Colonel St. George telling him that Sandwich had been abandoned without a fight. The General was rarely angry, but St. George's report displeased him extremely. This was not his way of waging war.

"By the Lord Harry," Brock exclaimed, "he has allowed the enemy to cross the river in open day without firing a shot!"

He also noted that St. George had waited three days before writing his dispatch. Obviously, so important a command as Amherstburg could not safely be left to St. George, and Brock at once sent Colonel Henry Procter to replace him.

The news from the west was bad. It was worrying to hear that large numbers of Canadian militiamen were deserting. True, only some of the deserters were sympathetic with the Americans. Most merely went home to bring in the harvest and would return to the colours when this was done. Being a fair-minded man, Brock knew there was some excuse for this type of deserter – to the poorer settlers, failure to bring in the harvest might mean a winter of starvation for their wives and children. What was more dangerous was the attitude of many people in the western part of Upper Canada: they were saying it was useless to resist the Americans with the few troops available.

The Indian tribes, not yet having heard of the capture of Michilimackinac, were still wavering in their loyalty. They might remain neutral. More likely, they might join the Americans in the hope of finding plunder on the winning side. This possibility naturally made the Canadian militiamen unwilling to march far from their homes, for fear they might come back to find them in ashes, with their families murdered.

When Brock returned to York on the 27th to open the Assembly, he found many of the legislators gloomy and defeatist. They refused to pass his proposed amendments to the Militia Act or to suspend habeas corpus during the emergency. Brock delivered a stirring speech which closed with these words: "We are engaged in an awful and eventful contest. By unanimity and dispatch in our councils, and by vigour in our operations, we may teach the enemy this lesson – that a country defended by free men, enthusiastically devoted to the cause of their king and constitution, can never be conquered!" This speech did something to encourage the down-hearted, but the General nevertheless dissolved the Assembly as soon as it had passed the money bills.

Brock knew, better than anyone, how little he had to fight with and how dangerous were the American armies on the frontiers, but he had no intention of revealing his private fears to those around him. As he did when William's bank had failed, Brock went about with a sunny face, pretending that all was well. If anything, he appeared more at his ease and more confident than ever. "I talk loud and look big," he jestingly wrote to Colonel Baynes at Quebec.

Assuming a carefree air was all the harder for Brock because he suffered a personal loss at about this time. His old servant, the faithful Private Dobson, who had stayed on as his batman past the usual age of retirement, fell ill. Dobson had the best of care, and each day the General visited the private soldier, bringing him little gifts and talking cheerfully of old times. But in spite of everything, Dobson grew daily weaker, until he finally fell into a coma and died. Brock was present at the death-bed, and when he left the sick-room for the last time his heart was grieved for a friend who had been with him more than twenty years.

The news of the capture of Michilimackinac reached Brock on July 29. He instantly wrote to Sir George Prevost, pointing out the advantages this victory would bring and hinting strongly that Captain Roberts should be promoted. Prevost ignored the hint and Roberts remained a captain, perhaps because he had attacked against Prevost's orders. However, the Governor-in-Chief claimed part of the credit for Roberts's success when he wrote to tell the good news to the British Secretary of State for War.

Although Brock did not know it, the situation was also improving around Detroit. One Indian had sworn never to make peace with the United States until the Indian lands in the West were safe for the tribes. Tecumseh, or "Crouching Panther", was a chief of the Shawnees who for the past two years had been trying to form an Indian confederation to resist the Americans. He and his brother, who was known as The Prophet, had built a settlement on the Tippecanoe River about 150 miles south-east of Fort Dearborn, now Chicago. The previous November, while Tecumseh had been in the far south agitating among the Indians there, an American army under General William Harrison had attacked and destroyed his town. After the Battle of Tippecanoe, Tecumseh had led the survivors to Upper Canada. He was now at Amherstburg, eager to strike a blow against the Americans. His chance was soon to come. On the night of August 5, Tecumseh, with a small raiding party of twenty-four braves, crossed the Detroit River to ambush an American force that was reported to be escorting mail from Fort Detroit. The eldest son of Colonel Matthew Elliott, the Superintendent of the Indian Department, disguised himself as an Indian and went along. When Tecumseh's scouts told him the Americans were approaching, the chief hid his little band in the thick woods on both sides of the road near Brownstown, twenty-five miles south of Detroit.

The early-morning mists were still clinging to the trees and covering the ground when 150 Ohio Volunteers under Major Thomas Van Horne came down the road without an advance-guard or skirmishers ahead of them. The soldiers had no warning that this stretch of road was any different from the miles they had covered safely the previous day. No branch stirred suspiciously among the green trees; no betraying gleam of metal showed in the thick underbrush along the roadside. On all sides there was nothing to see but the virgin forest of tall maples and poplars, lonely and serene in the fragrant morning air. The silence was broken only by the clop, clop of the horses' hooves, the steady tramp of the infantry, and the soldiers' voices as they talked together in the column.

The Indians lay concealed until the Americans were almost upon them. Then Tecumseh snapped out one word in his own language – "Fire!"

Twenty-six rifles blazed out together. Little puffs of blue smoke appeared briefly against the green foliage and the sharp smell of burnt gunpowder drifted down the air. In the American column two dozen men and horses went down with the first volley and the marching troops were thrown into wild confusion. When the Indians let out a war-whoop, the soldiers ran. Their officers tried vainly to re-form them; Van Horne's force did not reassemble until it was once again safely within the walls of Fort Detroit.

The Americans fled so quickly that most Indians had time to fire only once, but that fusillade killed seven officers and ten men and wounded twelve soldiers. Only one Indian was killed in Tecumseh's party. Word of the successful ambush at Brownstown spread quickly among the tribes and greatly increased Tecumseh's influence over his own people.

On August 6 Brock left York for the western frontier. When he had called for militia volunteers to accompany him, many more had stepped out than he could take with him. He selected 250 militiamen and with these and forty men of the 41st Regiment began his march. With him as his provincial aide-de-camp he took his friend Lieutenant-Colonel John Macdonell of Glengarry, the handsome young Attorney-General of Upper Canada, who was engaged to Susan Shaw's niece, Mary Powell.

The General travelled first to the Mohawk village on the Grand River where he was promised the help of sixty Indian braves. From there he marched to Long Point on Lake Erie and at once set about collecting shipping to

take his force to Amherstburg. From nearby farms he
soon rented ten open boats of the type the settlers used
for carrying their flour and other provisions. The boats
were heavy, awkward, and old; they were crudely put together; their planks were rotten; and they were dirty with
the accumulated dust and mould of years; but they were
the best that could be had. On the morning of August 8

Brock embarked his men and set sail up the coast.

With such boats Brock had to keep close inshore, following every twist and turn of the coastline, so that the voyage from Long Point to Amherstburg was fully 200 miles long. A sudden summer storm rose on the lake, whose shallow waters were quickly lashed into high waves; rain poured down; everyone was soaked to the skin, and the men were almost exhausted from having constantly to bail out the leaky boats; but Brock pressed on by night as well as by day, determined to strike at the invader as soon as possible. Each night when darkness fell, a pine torch soaked in resin was lighted and fixed to the stern of the General's boat to guide the rest of the little convoy. Even so, some of the ships had difficulty keeping station.

One afternoon, near Port Talbot, Brock's boat ran aground on a concealed reef. Although the boatmen struggled with oars and pike-poles, they were unable to get her off again. But the Guernsey-man, used to sailing small boats out of St. Peter's Port, stripped off his scarlet coat and his knee-length Hessian boots, vaulted over the side, and stood waist-deep in the water that covered the reef.

"Come on, lads," he called. "One good push and we'll have her free."

His soldiers, recovering from their surprise at suddenly seeing their General in the water, swarmed overside to join him on the reef, and the boat was soon afloat again.

Just after midnight on August 13, Brock's boat scraped up on the gravel beach at Amherstburg. The voyage from

Long Point had taken only five days. The General was greatly pleased with his men.

"In no instance have I seen troops who would have endured the fatigue of a long journey in boats during extremely bad weather, with greater cheerfulness and constancy," he said in his next Order-of-the-Day. "And it is but justice to this little band to add that their conduct throughout excited my admiration."

He could truthfully have added, too, that the soldiers felt exactly the same way about their General.

As Brock stepped ashore, Colonel Matthew Elliott, lean, grizzled, and looking rather like an Indian himself, was waiting on the beach to welcome him. Just then Brock heard a sharp rattle of musketry from the nearby island of Bois Blanc where the Indians were encamped. He turned and asked sharply:

"What is that firing, Colonel Elliott?"

Elliott explained that this was the Indians' way of welcoming their commander-in-chief.

Brock frowned. Powder was far too precious to be wasted in this manner. He explained this to Elliott and ordered that the firing should cease at once, but added:

"Do, pray, Elliott, fully explain my reason for this command, and tell the Indians that I will speak to them tomorrow."

General Brock was then escorted to Elliott's house which he was to make his temporary headquarters. As soon as Elliott saw that his guest was comfortable, he left to carry the General's message to the Indian chiefs.

While Elliott was gone, Colonel Procter and the other senior officers at Amherstburg told Brock what had occurred in the last few weeks. Brock was delighted to hear of Tecumseh's ambush at Brownstown and he was told of a skirmish near Maguaga that had ended in a British retirement. Three times the Americans had tried to cross the Canard River between Sandwich and Amherstburg, but each time they had been beaten off after light skirmishing. In one of these brushes with the enemy, two private soldiers of the 41st Regiment, Hancock and Dean, had displayed the greatest heroism when they had been left behind as sentries. The two men had been suddenly attacked by more than fifty Americans, but instead of running they had stood their ground. Hancock had been shot dead – the first British soldier to be killed in the war – and Dean had been knocked down by a musket-ball that snapped the bone in his upper arm. Struggling to his feet again, Dean had fought on, with his rifle and bayonet gripped in his one good hand, until he had been overwhelmed and captured.

Most important of all was the news that Hull, much against the wishes of his army, had abandoned Sandwich on August 7 and 8 and returned to Fort Detroit. The white-haired old general, who only a few days previously had been boasting of his overwhelming strength, now huddled within the walls of his fort nervously awaiting reinforcements. His soldiers were openly calling him a coward.

Brock was now given the mail Tecumseh had captured at Brownstown, and he discovered to his horror that the first scalping of the war had been the work, not of an Indian, but of a white man. A certain Captain William McCullough of Hull's army had written to his wife, boasting that after he had killed an Indian on the Canard River he had torn off the scalp with his teeth. However, the captured mail provided Brock with other, more pleasant information. There were hundreds of letters written by Hull's officers and soldiers, and all of them were filled with the same complaints. Although the men from Ohio had enjoyed the Canadian cider at Sandwich, they had lost all confidence in Hull and were near to mutiny. They wanted to attack Amherstburg at once, finish the war, and return home for the harvesting.

As well as the letters, there were two or three of Hull's own dispatches, and these showed that, instead of planning any attack, the American general was fearful of being cut off and attacked himself by the British on one hand and the Indians on the other. Brock smiled to himself as he read. It would be a pity to disappoint General Hull. Perhaps there was something he could do about that. . . .

While Brock was looking over the captured correspondence, Elliott returned with Tecumseh and a few other Indian chiefs – Roundhead, Splitlog, Warrow, and Walk-in-the-Water. The other chiefs hung back at the door while Tecumseh, their leader and spokesman, stepped forward.

When Tecumseh walked into the lamplight of Colonel Elliott's parlour, Brock, who was bending over a table littered with maps and letters, did not at once look up. The other officers saw that the Indian chief was of only medium height, but that he stood as straight as an arrow and had an easy grace of movement. They had an impression of a high forehead, a lean proud face, clear hazel eyes, and a resolute mouth – all immobile and impassive as though cast from bronze. The Indian was dressed in a fringed hunting frock of tanned buckskin, with buckskin leggings and moccasins. Three tiny silver coins hung down from his straight nose; he wore a large silver medallion of King George III around his neck on a coloured wampum string; and in his belt he carried a silver-mounted tomahawk and a hunting knife.

Then Brock raised his head and saw Tecumseh. Until now the General had had no very high opinion of his Indian allies. Although he sympathized with the wrongs they had suffered at the hands of the white man, he had found that many Indians were cruel, dissolute, and treacherous. Now, however, as he glanced sharply at Tecumseh, his eyes lit up and he slowly straightened. More than a quarter of a century of soldiering had taught him how to size up a man. He recognized, instantly and intuitively, that Tecumseh was one of his own kind, a fighter and a trustworthy comrade.

For his part, Tecumseh saw a huge man in a gold-laced scarlet coat, white breeches, and mirror-bright riding boots. He had seen many splendidly uniformed officers before without being in the least overawed, but Isaac Brock's character was plain on his face for the shrewd savage to read. Tecumseh saw courage, intelligence, honesty, and a kind firmness there, and knew that he was meeting a great man who was utterly without pretence.

A hush fell in the room as the British general and the Indian chief stood absolutely still and looked at each other. The silence seemed long, although it lasted only a few seconds. Then, as though some secret password had been exchanged, both men smiled deep in their eyes. Tecumseh turned to where the other chiefs stood in the shadows by the door. He made a slight gesture with his hand, indicating Brock.

"*This* is a man," he said.

Brock said nothing at the time, but the next day, in a letter to Lord Liverpool, the British Secretary of State for War, he wrote: "Among the Indians whom I found at Amherstburg, and who arrived from distant parts of the country, there are some extraordinary characters. He who most attracted my attention was a Shawnee Chief, Tecumseh, the brother of The Prophet, who for the last two years had carried on, contrary to our remonstrances, an active war against the United States. A more sagacious or a more gallant warrior does not, I believe, exist. He was the admiration of everyone who conversed with him."

Early on the morning of August 14, General Brock called together his senior officers and outlined the plan he had already formed. Although he had only some 700 soldiers and his Indian allies, he proposed nothing less than the immediate capture of Fort Detroit. Most of his officers were astounded. They were not used to such speed and boldness.

Colonel Procter, the second in command, protested vehemently against the General's plan.

"Fort Detroit is far too strong for us, sir," he said. "It

has dozens of guns – some of them big ones. And General Hull has more than 2,000 troops while we have less than 800. With all respect, sir, I think it would be madness to dream of attacking."

Lieutenant-Colonel St. George, too, was aghast at the idea. "We would have to fight our way ashore, sir," he urged, "and against very superior numbers. Once over, we would have our backs to the river."

Other officers also expressed their fears and disapproval. Of all those present, only the little Scottish storekeeper of Niagara, Robert Nichol, and the great-hearted Indian Chief Tecumseh agreed with Brock.

The General listened quietly to all the objections, but when everyone had had his say he stood up and spoke firmly but with perfect good humour:

"I have decided on crossing. And now, gentlemen, instead of any further advice, I entreat you to give me your cordial and hearty support."

After his senior officers had been dismissed, Brock next attended a full council of the Indian chiefs in their encampment on Bois Blanc Island. The General opened the council by saying that their great white father, the King, had ordered him to come to the Indians' aid and with their help to drive the Americans from Fort Detroit.

The Indians shouted their enthusiasm, and called on Tecumseh to reply.

The slender Shawnee Chief rose from his place and spoke briefly: "I have fought against the enemies of our great father, the King, beyond the Great Lakes, and they have never seen my back. I am come here to fight his enemies and now desire with my warriors to take lessons from you and your soldiers that we may learn how to make war in these deep forests."

When the council broke up, Brock took Tecumseh back to Colonel Elliott's house where he questioned him about the roads and streams on the American side of the Detroit River. Tecumseh drew his hunting knife and rapidly sketched a map of the area on a piece of flattened birch bark. The little map was as neat and accurate as if it had been drawn by a surveyor.

Brock had two more things to say to Tecumseh. He had heard that two American prisoners who had been captured in skirmishes had been murdered by the Indians. The Americans had been brought back to Bois Blanc Island, where they had at first been treated kindly and given food. Then, when they were off their guard, an Indian had crept up behind each man and split his skull with a tomahawk. Now Brock asked Tecumseh to promise that his warriors would henceforth observe the rules of war. There was to be no scalping, no torture, and no more killing of prisoners. Tecumseh gave his word and he kept it strictly. On one subsequent occasion he risked his own life to save an American prisoner his followers were about to murder.

Then Brock asked that Tecumseh's Indians "should not taste pernicious liquor until they had humbled the Big-Knives". The Shawnee Chief, who himself had long ago given up drinking, again promised to do as the General wished.

"If this resolution is persevered in," Brock said, "you must surely conquer."

After this, things moved fast. Brock divided his command into three brigades and appointed a number of captains, including his aide, John Glegg, to the local rank of major. On the suggestion of Major Thomas Evans, the brigade-major at Fort George, 350 discarded uniforms of the 41st Regiment had been sent to Amherstburg. They were shabby and worn out, but the scarlet coats were still bright. Brock now had these uniforms issued to the Canadian militia to deceive the Americans as to the number of regulars in the force.

Before daylight on August 15, Brock's little army was on the march to Sandwich. An American rear-guard of 250 men retired across the river without fighting as the British approached. As soon as he entered Sandwich, Brock had cannon hauled into emplacements for the bombardment of Fort Detroit. A British eighteen-gun sloop, the *Queen Charlotte*, and the armed brig *General Hunter*, of twelve guns, were sent up-river to cover the spot on the American shore where Brock proposed to land.

By noon on the 15th, just two days after Brock had landed at Amherstburg, his whole force, except for a weak garrison left at Amherstburg, had assembled opposite Fort Detroit, with guns in position and all arrangements made for an attack the following morning.

What speed and decision could do had been accomplished, but the attackers were, in fact, terribly weak. Brock had only 250 men of the 41st Regiment, fifty of the Royal Newfoundland Regiment, and some 400 militia – 700 white soldiers – and about 600 Indians. Now he remembered how, at Copenhagen, when Nelson's squadron

was lying badly battered in the roadsteads before the un-
damaged Danish forts, the indomitable English admiral
had coolly sent a summons for the enemy to surrender in
the name of humanity. Brock resolved to try the same
trick on General Hull.

A small boat put off from Sandwich early that afternoon, bearing Captain Glegg and Lieutenant-Colonel
Macdonell, Brock's two aides-de-camp. At the mast-head
of the little vessel there fluttered a white flag of truce. The
two aides were blindfolded and ushered into Fort Detroit,
but were not allowed to see General Hull. Brock's letter,
however, was delivered to the American commander.
The summons had been carefully worded to prey upon
the fears of the already frightened man. Brock had noted
Hull's dread of the Indians, and he guessed that, however
much he exaggerated the size and strength of his own
force, Hull's own timid imagination would incline him to
believe it.

General Brock's summons read:

Head-quarters, Sandwich,
August 15, 1812.

The force at my disposal authorises me to require of you
the immediate surrender of fort Detroit. It is far from my
intention to join in a war of extermination, but you must
be aware that the numerous body of Indians who have
attached themselves to my troops, will be beyond control
the moment the contest commences. You will find me
disposed to enter into such conditions as will satisfy the

most scrupulous sense of honour. Lieut-Colonel M'Donell and Major Glegg are fully authorised to conclude any arrangement that may lead to prevent the unnecessary effusion of blood.

Macdonell and Glegg were kept waiting for more than two hours before Hull made up his mind how to reply. When his answer finally came, it was a rejection of the demand to surrender.

Brock, of course, had expected this. The real purpose of his summons had been to frighten the American commander still further. Brock had studied his man, just as he had years ago in the Barbados when he had outfaced the quarrelsome duellist of the 49th Regiment. Both times the risk was actually less than it appeared because of the character of his opponent. Now, as soon as he received Hull's reply, he issued his orders. The attack would go in at dawn next day.

For an hour or two before sunset the British guns fired at the batteries across the river and the American guns replied. Neither bombardment did much damage, and as darkness closed in the guns fell silent; but all that night on Bois Blanc Island the Indian braves performed their war dances around great blazing fires. The flickering firelight reflected from nearly naked copper-coloured bodies painted bright vermilion, black and white, and purple. From the shadows around the fires war drums throbbed out a single deep note of menace and excitement, repeated maddeningly again and again until it seemed to enter the blood. The dancing braves brandished their tomahawks

and uttered piercing, high-pitched war-whoops.

General Brock did nothing to discourage this display of ferocity. The Detroit River at Sandwich is only three-quarters of a mile wide, and the noise of the Indian cele-

brations carried clearly across the water. In Fort Detroit
General Hull lay awake listening to it, tense and afraid,
but in Sandwich General Brock turned in early and slept
well.

7. The Fall of Detroit

BEFORE morning broke, the Indian braves on Bois Blanc Island slipped away from their camp-fires, crept silently down to the water's edge, and stepped into their war canoes. The paddles made no sound as the long birch-bark craft glided swiftly across the river. The savages landed as noiselessly as they had embarked. If there had been a watcher on the American shore, he would have glimpsed only a few shadows flitting among the trees. But there was no watcher. No American sentry heard the Indians come; no challenge rang out in the night. By daybreak Tecumseh had 600 warriors in position behind the line the Americans were to defend.

The bugler and drummer boys in Brock's army were up early on Sunday, August 16. The light was still grey and the air chilly when they sounded "Reveille" in the British lines. Men tumbled out of their blankets, stamping their feet and beating their arms to get the blood moving again after a night spent on the damp ground. They grinned at each other and made jokes – rather strained jokes, sometimes, for every soldier knew there might be bloody work to do before noon.

The General was up with the rest of them, walking

about the camp to see that everything was in good order. He watched the men folding up their bedding and making themselves ready for roll-call and inspection. He listened to the crisp commands of the sergeants and noticed with approval that as the companies marched off for breakfast they put a little extra swagger in their step when they passed where he was standing.

"Eyes – right!"

"Eyes front, please, sergeant!"

As he returned the salute, Brock smiled at his soldiers. They were just the men for the job at hand.

North of Sandwich on the river-bank, the British batteries had already opened fire again, the gunners stripped to the waist and sweating as they swabbed out their guns after each shot and hauled them back to the firing position after each recoil. The shooting yesterday had not been good, but this morning the gunners were aiming at Fort Detroit rather than at the American batteries, and the fort was a bigger target. It was hard to tell for certain so early in the morning, when the river was still covered with haze, but it looked as though the guns were getting the range today. Everyone was busy and everyone had some specific job to do, which was a good thing because busy men have little time to be frightened.

In Fort Detroit the atmosphere was very different. The officers and men of the North West Army had no idea what might happen next or what might be expected of them. They had been crowded inside the palisades and then left to do pretty much as they liked. No one inspected them to see that they had shaved or that their uniforms were smart and their brass polished. No one looked down the barrels of their rifles or insisted that their boots be shone. They had not enough work to keep them from listening to rumours, and they were given no definite orders. The colonels from Ohio had already discussed putting General Hull under arrest – of the four senior officers only Lieutenant-Colonel Miller, the regular soldier, any longer even pretended to treat him with courtesy – but apart from their mutinous grumblings, which they did not trouble to hide from the men, the Ohio colonels had done nothing.

At sunset on August 14, General Hull had sent out a detachment of 400 men under colonels McArthur and Cass to escort a provisions train into Detroit. But the next day, after receiving Brock's summons to surrender, Hull had dispatched an officer on a fast horse with urgent orders for the party to return. The message had been delivered safely, but on the morning of the 16th there was still no sign of McArthur and his 400 men.

Hull himself was nearly in a state of nervous exhaustion. Ever since his march through the Black Swamp, he had grown each day more silent and withdrawn. Now he issued most of his orders through his son and his son-in-law. On the rare occasions when he did meet any of his officers or men he appeared to be "sullen in his deportment and wavering in his decisions".

When the British guns had opened fire the previous afternoon, he had come close to panic.

"My God! What shall I do with the women and children?" he had exclaimed, perhaps remembering that his own daughter and her children were in the fort with him.

In fact, there were only a few officers' families at Detroit and most of them were safely sheltered in a stone root cellar in a nearby orchard. A few of the wives, more spirited than the commanding general, insisted on remaining in the fort to sew powder bags for the guns.

The British artillerymen had been right in thinking that they had the range of Fort Detroit. Soon after breakfast a cannon-ball shrieked over the rampart, landed on the parade ground, ricocheted off, and killed a private soldier.

At six o'clock in the morning the British and Canadians began to cross the river in a fleet of assorted small craft. General Brock stood erect in the bow of one of the leading boats, so that all might see him and draw confidence from his familiar figure. By now the sun was well up in a cloudless sky and the day was already hot. Out from the American shore, where their guns could cover the landing, the *Queen Charlotte* and *General Hunter* rode at anchor.

As it turned out, the naval guns were not needed. When Brock's force landed at Spring Wells, some three miles west of Fort Detroit, not an American soldier was in sight.

Once all the troops were disembarked, General Brock ordered the muster-rolls to be called. When the final report came in, he found he had 730 soldiers with him. He had intended to take up a position near the fort in the hope that Hull might come out to attack him, but while the five light field-guns he had ferried across the river were still being unloaded, Tecumseh and Matthew Elliott approached him. With them was an Indian scout who for the past several days had been roaming the countryside about Detroit. With Colonel Elliott interpreting for him, the Indian told how he had come upon a large number of Americans encamped in the forest three miles away. This was Colonel McArthur's detachment of 400 Ohio Volunteers who were still showing no sign of obeying Hull's orders to return.

"Last night before the sun went down they made camp," the Indian said. "This morning they made big fires. Now they are roasting oxen over the fires and eating them."

Brock turned to Colonel Elliott. "Ask him if the Americans did not hear the gun-fire this morning."

The scout shrugged his naked shoulders. "They hear the guns. But they are eating first before they march."

On the instant Brock decided to attack the fort itself and carry it by storm while its garrison was still under-strength. He issued his orders quickly but with the calm cheerfulness he always displayed in the presence of the enemy. His staff leapt to obey him. The red-coated soldiers were at once formed up on the road that ran alongside the river, and in a matter of minutes the little army was on the march. Double the normal distance was left between sections so that the marching column would look larger than it actually was.

A company of the 41st Regiment under Lieutenant Bullock led the way, and behind this advance-guard came the three six-pounder and the two three-pounder field-guns, each pulled by a team of horses. Ahead of the column the white road wound gently uphill to Fort Detroit. Occasionally through the trees the soldiers could catch glimpses of its weathered palisades, looking very solid and menacing in the bright sunlight. Close on the column's right the blue river shimmered in the August heat, and on its left the road was bounded by a line of rail fences and a few log farmhouses. As the troops swung into a steady, rhythmic stride, their boots kicked up a low cloud of white dust which marked their progress across the sun-drenched countryside.

About a mile from Spring Wells and two miles from the fort, the road straightened and the soldiers could see some distance ahead. A few hundred yards in front of them a ravine crossed their path and ran down to the river. And there, on the far side of the ravine, plainly visible through the clear air and pointing straight down the road at the advancing soldiers, stood two huge twenty-four-pounder guns.

Their muzzles looked enormous, like two black caverns. American gunners were clustered behind each cannon and the gun-sergeants stood with their yard-long matches burning in their hands. Each red-coated soldier knew that, once those matches were touched to the fuse-holes, a storm of grape-shot would tear the head of the column to bits.

Not one of the marching men faltered. The sweat on their foreheads felt suddenly cold and their stomach muscles tightened, but they tramped steadily on through the heat and the dust. Up at the head of the column strode the tall figure of General Brock, very conspicuous

in his cocked hat and decorated general's coat. And where the General led, every man was determined to follow.

The sight of Brock in a position of such obvious danger was too much for his old friend, Lieutenant-Colonel

Nichol. The little Scotsman came running up the side of
the column, saluted, and fell into step at the General's
side. Then, a little breathlessly, he began to remonstrate
with him.

"Pardon me, General, but I must beg you not to expose yourself like this. If we lose you, we lose everything. Let me pray you to allow the troops to pass on, led by their own officers."

Brock looked down with a smile.

"Master Nichol, I appreciate the advice you give me," he said, "but I feel that in addition to their sense of loyalty and duty many here follow me from a feeling of personal regard, and I will never ask them to go where I do not lead them."

Brock continued along the road for another hundred yards, drawing nearer and nearer to the deadly guns. Then, just as Tecumseh's birch-bark map had told him would be the case, he came upon a lane running off to the left where the soldiers could find shelter from fire. Stepping out of the column, he stood in the middle of the road, his back turned carelessly on the American gunners, and watched while the troops wheeled past him to turn down this lane and take up a covered position in a field and orchard. Each man, as he passed safely out of the line of fire, felt the tension drain out of him and the day grow warm again.

At the General's order, the regimental officers began to shake out their troops into line for the assault. While this was going on, Brock went forward and personally inspected the fort to choose the best point of attack. The five field-guns were hauled into position to give supporting fire, and a rifle company was sent far out to the left to make contact with Tecumseh's Indians in the woods.

In Fort Detroit, General Hull was already a broken

man. Brock's advance had been reported to him, and he
had been told that every one of the attacking soldiers wore
the scarlet coat of a British regular. He had heard, too,
that Tecumseh's Indians were moving about in the surrounding forest, and his fearful imagination convinced
him that he was about to be assailed by at least 5,000
savages. He had forbidden his guns to fire, giving as an
excuse that he wanted to save powder, although his real
reason would seem to have been a dread of opening the
battle. Now he ordered all his outlying troops back into
the fort. Even here he did not feel secure.

Yet he was in a very strong position. Fort Detroit, which
covered about an acre of ground, was protected by a high
palisade, a twenty-six-foot rampart with four bastions,
and a glacis.* A ditch, six feet deep and twelve feet wide,
ran around the entire fort. Hull had over forty cannon,
including three ten-inch howitzers, and a plentiful supply
of ammunition. Even though the 400-man detachment
under McArthur and Cass had not returned, he had 1,700
soldiers, more than double the number Brock had. Hull
must have known, too, that Indians, although excellent
fighters in their native forests, were seldom of any use in
an attack on a fortified place. In the Peninsula, British,
French, and Spanish garrisons had all successfully defended weaker fortifications for weeks.

The British shelling from across the river now intensi-
fied. One mortar bomb crashed through the roof of the
officers' mess-hall and burst inside, killing four officers,
one of whom was Lieutenant Hanks, on parole after the

*A bank, sloping down from a fort, on which attackers are exposed to fire.

surrender of Fort Michilimackinac. The mess-hall was turned into a charnel house, with blood and bits of bodies splattered on all four walls. When General Hull saw this, his fear grew.

Now, too, Hull heard that the Michigan militia were deserting their posts. Civilians from the town, who had sought refuge within the fort, were running about in panic, getting in the way of the troops. And when Hull's son ordered a company of Ohio Volunteers, who were loitering in the street, to join their comrades at the palisades, they refused to obey him. He drew his sword on the men, but their officer intervened and Captain Hull promptly challenged him to a duel. The prospect of his son's being killed by a militia officer worried the fearful Hull.

At ten o'clock Hull ordered his son to run up a white flag, not with the purpose of surrendering the fort but to arrange a parley with Brock. Captain Hull was about to haul down the Stars and Stripes and hoist a white towel in its place when a senior officer interfered. The towel, he said, was disgracefully dirty. Moreover, to run up a white flag in place of the American ensign would signify the complete surrender of the fort. Finally a bed-sheet was procured and draped over the south-western bastion.

While this was being done, Captain Hull set out across the Detroit River in a row-boat under a flag of truce. He carried the following message for General Brock: "I propose a cessation of hostilities for one hour to open negotiations for the surrender of Detroit – W. M. Hull, B. Gen."

General Hull had little idea what manner of man his opponent was. Brock was certainly not at his headquarters in Sandwich. When Hull's son crossed the river in search of him, the British general was actually within a few hundred yards of Fort Detroit, well ahead of his army, reconnoitring the ramparts without an escort.

At length, however, Hull's message was delivered to Brock, who sent Macdonell and Glegg into Fort Detroit to arrange a surrender. Brock insisted that his terms be agreed to within three hours. Otherwise he would at once proceed with the assault.

In less than an hour Macdonell and Glegg returned to the British lines with word that Hull had agreed to all Brock's demands. The two aides reported that the American general was in a pitiable condition, his voice faltering and his hands trembling. He had been chewing tobacco to calm his nerves, and his lips, chin, and neckcloth had been stained with tobacco juice. Hull had especially requested that Colonel McArthur's 400 men be included in the surrender, because he believed that if they tried to fight their way to safety they would be massacred by the Indians.

Brock refused to grant the American garrison the privilege of marching out of Fort Detroit with the customary honours of war. Although he was glad enough to win a complete victory without bloodshed, his soldierly spirit was outraged by so shameful a capitulation. He always had the greatest respect for brave enemies, but to grant General Hull the honours of war would have been only a mockery.

The American troops shared Brock's contempt for their general, and were much more ready to give it expression. Many of them raged in helpless fury when told to lay down their arms without fighting. When by mistake the British honour guard under Lieutenant Bullock marched into the fort sooner than the terms of surrender allowed, the Ohio Volunteers looked very fierce and angry. An ugly incident could easily have occurred, but the guard was promptly marched out again before trouble developed.

At noon the American soldiers stacked their arms and filed sullenly from the fort. Some of the men smashed their rifles rather than turn them in, and when Colonel Cass returned to find the fort surrendered he snapped his sword across his knee and cried.

The British marched in when the Americans marched out. The American flag was hauled down and the Union Jack broken out in its place, while the red-coated honour guard stood rigidly at attention. A military band struck up "God Save the King", the soldiers presented arms with a flourish, and a salute was fired from a recaptured British cannon which had originally been taken in the American Revolutionary War.

While the prisoners were being sorted out and an inventory made of the captured stores, General Brock went at once to the fort's guard-room where he personally released Private Dean of the 41st Regiment, the soldier who had fought so bravely on the Canard River the previous month. The General shook Dean by the hand and said in front of everyone:

"I'm very glad to have you back with us, Private Dean. You are a credit to your regiment and to the service."

Brock then went out to the square, sat down on a gunpowder barrel, and wrote a brief dispatch to Sir George Prevost:

Hd.Quarters, Detroit
August 16th 1812

Sir,

I hasten to apprize Your Excellency of the Capture of this very important Post – 2500 troops have this day surrendered Prisoners of war, and about 25 pieces of Ordnance have been taken, without the sacrifice of a drop of British blood.

I had not more than 700 troops including Militia and about 600 Indians to accomplish this service – When I detail my good fortune Your Excellency will be astonished – I have been admirably supported by Colonel Procter, the whole of my staff and I may justly say every individual under my Command.

Believe me,
Your Ex's faithful obedient
Humble Servant
Isaac Brock, M.G.

Brock was only a little out in his initial calculation of the number of prisoners taken at Fort Detroit. When they were counted, they were found to number 2,338. But when the captured guns were counted there proved to be 39 of them, in addition to the fixed pieces on the walls. The colours of the 4th United States Infantry were rescued from the hands of an American private soldier who was courageously attempting to burn them. Tecumseh's braves were especially overjoyed at the capture of this trophy, for it had been the 4th U.S. Infantry that had destroyed their village of Tippecanoe.

As soon as Brock had written his dispatch to Sir George Prevost, he dashed off a hurried little letter to his brothers on Guernsey: "My dear Brothers and Friends, – Rejoice at my good fortune, and join me in prayers to Heaven. I send you a copy of my hasty note to Sir George. Let me hear that you are all *united* and happy."

General Hull and his regular soldiers were shipped to Montreal where they were held until they were exchanged or paroled. The married American officers, with their wives and families, were sent to Newark, and the Ohio Volunteers, after they had given their parole, were allowed to make their own way home as best they could. When General Hull eventually returned to the United States he was court-martialled for treason and cowardice, found guilty on the latter charge, and sentenced to be shot. President Madison, however, commuted the sentence because of Hull's age and his former services to the Republic. The old general spent the rest of his life trying to justify his actions.

Tecumseh's braves had behaved admirably at Fort Detroit, and General Brock made a point of telling them so. Later in the day when he and Tecumseh met inside the fort, the General took off his scarlet sash and presented it to the Indian as a token of friendship. Tecumseh's eyes lit up at the gift, partly in child-like pleasure at receiving so bright an ornament, but more because it came from such a man.

The next morning Tecumseh appeared without the sash, and Brock, worried that he might accidentally have done something to hurt the Chief's feelings, asked him where it was.

"I gave it to Chief Roundhead," Tecumseh replied. "He is an older and more experienced warrior than I. While he was here, I could not think of wearing such a badge of distinction."

It is no wonder that Tecumseh had such great influence over all the tribes!

One frontier was now safe for the time being, but no sooner had Fort Detroit been captured than Brock was fretting to get back to the Niagara River where another American army was massing for invasion. He left Colonel Procter in charge at Detroit and before dawn on August 18 set sail on the schooner *Chippawa*. With him went seventy prisoners and, as a guard, a rifle company commanded by Captain John Beverley Robinson of the York militia.

Brock drew the younger man into conversation during the voyage, and they spent several hours together. Robinson later recalled one significant thing the General had said. One evening, leaning over the after-rail of the schooner and watching her wake bubble and fade in the blue water, Brock said musingly:

"If this war lasts, I am afraid that I shall do some foolish thing, for if I know myself there is no want of courage in my nature – I hope I shall not get into a scrape."

The mood lasted only a moment. Brock straightened up and at once began to talk lightly of some other topic, but before two months were out Captain Robinson was to have good reason to remember his general's words.

8. On the Niagara Frontier

On the morning of August 23, the *Chippawa* was beating up the eastern end of Lake Erie against a light wind when the *Lady Prevost*, an armed schooner of fourteen guns, hove into view. Signal flags broke out at the mast-heads of both ships, and, when the *Lady Prevost*'s captain learned that the *Chippawa* had General Brock aboard, he ordered his gunners into action. The schooner's gun-ports opened; the black muzzles of her cannon poked out; and the crash of gun-fire echoed across the lake. The President of Upper Canada was getting a seventeen-gun salute.

Brock probably felt that this was a waste of powder – it was a subject on which he had decided views – but as soon as the last gun had fired, a fresh string of flags fluttered out from the *Lady Prevost*'s forepeak: "*Heave to. Our Captain wishes to come aboard.*"

Brock waited impatiently in his cabin for the captain. The naval officer would have a good reason for requesting an interview. Perhaps he carried news of another American invasion, this time across the Niagara or St. Lawrence river.

The captain's news was worse than that. The Governor-in-Chief, Sir George Prevost, had concluded an armistice

with the American commander-in-chief, General Dearborn.

As soon as Prevost had heard of the repeal of the orders-
in-council that President Madison claimed caused the
war, he had sent his adjutant-general, Colonel Baynes, to
the United States to arrange a cease-fire. General Dearborn, who needed extra time to organize his armies,
quickly agreed. The armistice had gone into effect on
August 9.

General Brock could not conceal his regret and chagrin
at the naval officer's news. It would, of course, be senseless to carry on the war if the Americans really intended
to make peace, but Brock, who had lived in Canada much
longer than Prevost, did not believe the War Hawks would
so easily give up their dreams of conquering all North
America. An armistice at this time seemed dangerously
unwise.

Canada could only be defended if time were gained by
raids that would upset American preparations. Now would
have been the time to strike hard in the centre, at Fort
Niagara, and at the growing American naval base at
Sackett's Harbour on Lake Ontario. Before he had embarked on the *Chippawa*, Brock had sent Captain Glegg
to report in person to Sir George Prevost at Montreal and
to present him with the captured colours of the 4th U.S.
Infantry Regiment. Brock's last words to Glegg had been:

"You may inform Sir George that I intend immediately
to attack the naval arsenal at Sackett's Harbour. And you
may expect to hear of my arrival at Kingston soon after
you reach Montreal."

The armistice was doubly unfortunate, because the capture of Detroit was already having a tremendous effect in Upper Canada. The Canadians felt a fresh surge of confidence, and even the Six Nations, who had hitherto remained neutral, now declared for Brock. The country could be defended after all – and with such a commander as Brock it surely would be.

At Fort George, which he reached on August 24, Brock received dozens of congratulatory letters from friends and well-wishers, but each day, under cover of the armistice, General Dearborn steadily reinforced the Niagara frontier. Men, guns, stores, and equipment moved in ceaselessly to strengthen the American commander, Stephen Van Rensselaer. Every day troops could be seen moving on the roads leading to Lewiston and Buffalo. In the open fields across the river the white canvas of new tent-lines often sprang up overnight like mushrooms on a lawn. Tell-tale mounds of fresh earth showed where new batteries had been dug for American guns.

Most afternoons Brock would ride along the river road and look at these preparations. Often he would dismount, throw the reins over Alfred's head, and stand for a long time on the Canadian shore, watching the enemy's ominous activity through his big brass telescope. The Americans certainly meant to attack soon. Sir George Prevost, however, worried about the safety of Montreal and, in spite of Colonel Baynes's assurances that the men could be spared, bluntly refused to send Brock reinforcements.

Less than a week after he reached Fort George, Brock was again on board ship, this time bound for Kingston to inspect the local militia. It is said that before he sailed he met his fiancée, Susan Shaw, in Niagara and was able to spend some hours with her. During the five-day voyage to Kingston he wrote a long letter to his brothers, giving them the good news that he would now be able to save his family from the financial trouble caused by the failure of William's bank: "It is supposed that the value of the articles captured [at Detroit] will amount to £30 or £40,000," he wrote. "In that case, my proportion will be something considerable. If it enables me to contribute to your comfort and happiness, I shall esteem it my highest reward."

Then he touched on a matter far more important to him than the money. "Let me know, my dearest brothers, that you are all united again. The want of union was nearly losing this province without even a struggle, and be assured it operates in the same degree in regard to families."

The letter ended rather sadly. The long years of war against Napoleon were taking their toll and Brock had lost many of his friends and comrades. "I begin to be too old to form new friendships," he wrote, "and those of my youth are dropping off fast."

He had been in Kingston less than two hours when he received word that President Madison had rejected Prevost's armistice. The repeal of the orders in council had not been enough to ensure peace; the eyes of the War Hawks still glittered with the hope of winning all Canada. The war was to begin again in four days.

General Brock hurried back to Fort George, but once there he could do little but wait to be invaded. Sir George

Prevost still insisted that no attack be made on the Americans. When there had been some hope of peace, this attitude had been understandable, but now Prevost's orders made no sense at all.

Perhaps because his hint about the promotion of Captain Roberts had been ignored, Brock asked more definitely that Prevost promote Captain Glegg, pointing out that his merit and length of service gave him a powerful claim. The Governor-in-Chief could not very well disregard this request and Glegg was made a brevet-major. However, when the aide-de-camp reached Montreal, he was received coldly, and when Prevost wrote to the British Secretary of State for War he claimed some of the credit for Brock's victory at Detroit – in spite of the fact that Brock had actually captured Detroit after Prevost's armistice had gone into effect. Worse than this, in an Order-of-the-Day published August 31, Prevost practically apologized to the Americans because Brock had pursued General Hull's invading army into the United States.

The tone of the correspondence between Brock and the Governor-in-Chief now became increasingly stiff, although Brock was always polite and respectful. On September 14, Prevost wrote in a panic and ordered Brock to evacuate Fort Detroit and the whole Michigan territory adding once again that he could send no reinforcements to Upper Canada. Brock replied that, since Prevost had left him some latitude, he would not abandon Detroit just yet. He added a strong plea that if peace were made, his Indian allies should be treated fairly.

On October 6 in London, England, William Brock and

his wife Sally were awakened by the sound of bells ringing and guns booming out in salute. When his wife asked him what could be the reason for the celebration, William jokingly answered that it was for Isaac, since this was his forty-third birthday. Much to his surprise he found later in the day that the noise had indeed been for Isaac – word had just been received of the capture of Detroit.

The Prince Regent was so pleased with the victory that he at once appointed Brock a Knight of the Most Honourable Order of the Bath. Henceforth he would be Sir Isaac Brock. The news of Detroit and Isaac's appeals for family unity also led William and Irving to be reconciled. They met on Guernsey on October 13 and shook hands.

Meanwhile, the American army on the Niagara River was becoming daily larger and more menacing. General Van Rensselaer now had some 6,300 men to throw against Brock's 1,500, and Van Rensselaer could choose his point of attack.

In a daring raid on the night of October 8, an American cutting-out party in two long-boats slipped silently along-side the British vessels *Detroit* and *Caledonia* right under the guns of Fort Erie. The Americans, armed with cutlasses and pistols, swarmed aboard, quickly subdued the crews, cut the cables, and sailed the two ships out of the harbour. The *Detroit* ran aground and had to be set afire to prevent her recapture, but the *Caledonia* survived to serve well under Commodore Perry the following year.

Brock rode hard to Fort Erie when he heard of this disaster, but it was too late to save the ships. The commander of Fort Erie had certainly been careless and the General replaced him. Prevost's orders not to strike back vexed Brock more and more every day. He wrote to the Governor-in-Chief: "I shall refrain as long as possible, under your excellency's positive injunctions, from every hostile act, although sensible that each day's delay gives [the enemy] a positive advantage."

Yet, the same day, in a letter to Colonel Procter, Brock could still find excuses for Prevost's weakness: "Were it not for the positive injunctions of the commander of the forces," he wrote, "I should have acted with greater decision. This forbearance may be productive of ultimate good, but I doubt its policy – but perhaps we have not the means of judging correctly. You will of course adopt a very different line of conduct. The enemy must be kept in a state of constant ferment."

This was typical of him: an officer who knew him well for many years said that Brock never uttered a malicious word about anyone.

Along the Niagara frontier the initiative was left to the Americans. On the night of October 10, General Van Rensselaer brought thirteen big boats up to Lewiston from the Falls by wagon. He intended to attack Queenston that night and had actually embarked his troops when he discovered that the leading boat, commanded by a Lieutenant Sims, had disappeared – and that Sims's boat contained all the oars. The American soldiers had to be marched back to their barracks and the invasion postponed. Sims's boat was found abandoned down-river the next day, but Sims himself was never heard of again.

Nevertheless, an attack would have to come soon. Before long the rains and frosts of autumn would force Van Rensselaer to disperse his poorly clothed and badly sheltered army. Moreover, the American general had just received a false report from a spy that Brock had left for Detroit with most of his regular troops.

The night of October 12 was filled with wind and rain.

Thunder cracked and rolled across the river, and every few minutes the world was lit up with the blue glare of lightning. The storm beat against the windows of the office in Fort George where Brock was working late at his desk. He was writing a final dispatch to Sir George Prevost:

"The vast number of troops which have been this day

added to the strong force previously collected on the opposite side convinces me, with other indications, that an attack is not far distant. . . ."

Brock signed his name, sprinkled a few grains of sand on the paper to blot the ink, then rose and stretched himself. By now it was long past midnight and the storm was wilder than ever. It was time to go to bed.

He slept soundly until four o'clock in the morning, then – suddenly – he was wide awake. It was still dark and the rain was still slashing against the windows. But it was not the thunderstorm that had awakened him. He lay in bed, listening.

Then he heard it again, the sound that had penetrated his sleep. Guns were firing to southward. The attack he had been expecting had come.

9. A Hero's Death

JUMPING out of bed, Brock went to the window and opened the casement. The rain spattered in, cold against his face, but the noise of gun-fire from up-river was distinct above the sounds of the storm. As he listened, Brock thought he could distinguish the boom-boom-boom of the four-gun American battery at Lewiston and the slower reply of the British eighteen-pounder on Queenston Heights. Another gun was firing somewhat closer to Fort George. That would be the Half-Moon Battery at Vrooman's Point. There was cause for satisfaction in this. At least his outposts did not seem to have been taken by surprise.

He called for his servant, Private Thomas Porter, who since the summer had been doing his best to take Dobson's place. When Porter appeared, Brock was already dressing. He sent the man running to the stables with orders to rouse the grooms. Alfred was to be saddled and at his door within a quarter of an hour.

As Brock pulled on his boots he gave brisk commands to Major Glegg, who had been summoned to his bedroom.

"Have the garrison stand to at once, John," he said.

"Wake General Sheaffe and tell him I've gone to investigate. He must get the troops ready to march but tell him not to set them in motion just yet. I will send him a message if I want them. And wake Macdonell for me, John. You can follow on yourself once you are finished here."

Brock remembered the ridiculous attempt of the Americans against Queenston two nights previously. Even raw militiamen, commanded by political generals and elected officers, would surely have done better than that if they had been in earnest. It could have been nothing more than a feint, an attempt to make him draw off troops towards Queenston so that the real attack could be launched directly against Fort George.

In any case, the General intended to see for himself. Some twenty minutes after he had awakened to the sound of gun-fire, he was mounted on Alfred. The sentries at the main gate recognized the big grey horse that came prancing across the square, but the guard scarcely had time to turn out before the General was level with them. He saluted punctiliously from the saddle, then he was out of the fort and off down the Queenston road, riding hard in the wild October darkness, his cloak streaming out behind him in the north-east wind and the rain driving against his left side.

Up-stream at Queenston, the first of the Americans had already begun to cross the Niagara River. The thirteen big boats had been assembled again at Lewiston, and at three o'clock in the morning a column of 300 New York militia under Colonel Solomon Van Rensselaer, the General's relative and Chief of Staff, and another column

of 300 regulars under Lieutenant-Colonel John Chrystie
had started to embark. The moonless night, the storm,
and the need for silence all slowed the loading of the
boats.

Between Lewiston and Queenston the Niagara River is
only 200 yards wide, but its swift eddies and treacherous
currents, combined with the darkness, caused three of the
boats to go astray. Lieutenant-Colonel Chrystie and most
of the regulars were in these boats, which were carried
down-stream past the intended point of landing. The remaining ten, however, were rowed across towards the
Canadian shore.

On the Canadian side there were very few troops, only
about 300 men in all. The light company of the 49th
Regiment under Captain John Williams was half-way
down the slope of Queenston Heights near the Redan
Battery, an open, V-shaped fortification for the protection
of the single eighteen-pounder gun mounted within.
Captain John Chisholm's company of the York Volunteers was stationed a little further down the hillside. The
other flank company of the 49th, the Grenadier Company
commanded by Major James Dennis, was in the village
of Queenston itself, but it contained only forty-six men.
Captain Samuel Hatt's Company of the 5th Lincoln
Battalion was doing outpost duty along the river-bank.
Lieutenant William Crowther of the 41st Regiment had
a detachment of two light, three-pounder "grass-hopper"
guns in Queenston.

Down by the river-bank the Canadian sentries were
alert and nervous. There were too few militiamen for the

stretch of frontier to be patrolled, so each sentry had a long, lonely beat. It was an eerie job, too, especially when the storm raged through the forest, stripping the brown and scarlet leaves from the trees and filling the night with strange noises.

The little squares of mellow lamplight that were the windows of Queenston had long since blinked out one by one. High above the village loomed the black mass of the Queenston escarpment, running inland to the west at right-angles to the river. The chilly rain beat down, causing the sentries to huddle in their greatcoats and think longingly of the fire waiting for them in the guard-house. Below the foot-path where the sentries walked, the river itself was a dark shadow, marked here and there with touches of white foam.

At first the sentry whose beat was just below the village thought he was imagining what he saw. He stopped and peered out across the river into the darkness, his heart beating faster and a cold shiver running up the back of his neck. Out in the gloom of the swift-flowing water he could just make out a shadowy outline – a boat loaded to the gunwales with armed men! He could catch the dull gleam of their rifle barrels and the glint of their equipment. And there, behind the first boat, was another – and another – and another. The Americans were coming!

Instead of firing his musket and raising a general alarm, the sentry, after one hoarse cry, turned and ran. He bolted back up the path to the guard-house, stumbling in the blackness and sobbing a little in his haste and excitement. At the guard-house it took a minute or two to convince the sergeant that a landing was actually taking place, but then the defenders moved rapidly.

The Grenadier Company of the 49th was soon under arms and moving out from Queenston to attack the invaders. With them came the two grasshopper guns, bouncing lightly along over the rough road. The militiamen on the river-bank had already opened a ragged musketry fire, and the American gunners in the Lewiston battery, hearing this and knowing that surprise had been lost, began their own cannonade. American case-shot was soon spraying the Canadian bank to the right and left of the point of landing, but although it was unpleasant this firing did no harm.

From their vantage-point half-way up Queenston Heights the twelve gunners who served the eighteen-pounder cannon in the Redan Battery could make out the dim shapes of some American boats in midstream. One of the gun-crew snatched the canvas muzzle-cover from the end of the long barrel, while the officer in charge of the detachment trained the gun on the leading boat. The bow of the boat loomed darkly in the V of the fore-sight, the officer depressed the gun a fraction of an inch; then his hand came down smartly to slap his thigh – "Fire!"

The gunners swung away and covered their ears as the eighteen-pounder went off with a roar. Far out on the dark river three dozen balls of grape-shot whined through the air and struck the leading boat amidships. The gunners heard the screams and cries of wounded men come faintly across the water, but they had no time to pause and listen.

"Run up!" snapped the officer, and the gun-crew jumped to get the eighteen-pounder back to the firing position. "Load!" As they rammed home the powder bags, they heard the twenty-four-pounder carronade at Vrooman's Point, which also commanded a portion of the river,

fire its first round. It was a very welcome sound.

By now the first wave of invaders had landed. Colonel
Van Rensselaer was trying to form them into line when
the Grenadier Company and the grasshopper guns arrived
and opened fire. It had suddenly developed into a very

lively morning at the little village of Queenston.

Brock had ridden only some three miles along the Queenston road when he met a horseman coming at full gallop from the opposite direction. As the two riders flashed past each other in the darkness, Brock saw that the other man was Lieutenant S. P. Jarvis of Captain Duncan Cameron's flank company of the York Volunteers, which had been stationed on guard duty at Brown's Point about half-way between Queenston and Fort George.

As he went by, Jarvis shouted out for the General to halt, but the wind caught his words and whirled them away. In any case, Brock had no intention of stopping. With some difficulty the lieutenant reined in his restive horse, wheeled, and went after the General. He caught up with him about half a mile further along the road, and the two men rode together side by side while Jarvis told Brock of the attack on Queenston.

Brock listened carefully. Occasionally, at a bend in the road, he could see the musket-flashes along the Canadian shore and the reflected gleams on the water where the American reinforcements were firing from their boats. This was no feint, but a landing in force. He issued his orders without checking Alfred's steady pace. Jarvis was to ride to Fort George as fast as his horse would carry him and order General Sheaffe to march on Queenston at once with every available man. A party of friendly Indians who were encamped near the fort were to be sent as scouts to the woods on the west of the road to cover Sheaffe's flank during his advance.

Jarvis saluted and turned his horse once more towards

Fort George. He had not gone far before he met Colonel Macdonell galloping headlong down the road. The latter was in a desperate hurry to catch up with his General, for he would have considered it a stain on his honour to have been left behind when his friend and superior rode into action. General Brock had already left the fort when Macdonell had been awakened. The colonel had thrown on his clothes and run to the stables where sleepy grooms were saddling his big mare. Within minutes of waking, Macdonell had been in the saddle and on the road. Only after he was well away from Fort George had he realized that he had come without his sword.

"I would be much obliged to you, Mr. Jarvis, if you would lend me yours," Colonel Macdonell said, eyeing the blade at Jarvis's side. "You may take mine from my quarters in exchange."

Jarvis unbuckled his sword and passed it over. Macdonell grasped it and, without waiting to strap it on, thanked Jarvis, dug his spurs into his mare, and was off again down the road.

As soon as Captain Cameron of the York Volunteers had heard the gun-fire from the American shore he had called his company to arms. While the men were mustering, an officer had arrived from Queenston to report that large numbers of Americans were landing and to request that Cameron's company march at once to help oppose them. Accordingly, after having sent Lieutenant Jarvis off to Fort George to notify General Brock, Cameron ordered his company to fall in and marched it towards the battlefield.

Brock cantered past Brown's Point, and a little farther on came upon Captain Cameron's men stepping out briskly down the road. With a cheerful wave of his hand, the General called out to their captain:

"That's right, Captain Cameron. Hurry on the brave York Volunteers."

The twenty-four-pounder carronade at Vrooman's Point was in action as Brock rode by. The first grey light of dawn was now breaking, but the muzzle-flashes of the big gun were still a vivid orange brightness every time a round was fired. Captain Heward's company from Little York was encamped near the Half-Moon Battery, and Brock ordered it forward. As he was doing so, Colonel Macdonell, his horse almost blown, pulled up alongside him. A few minutes later Major Glegg joined Macdonell and the General on the road.

The battle was not going well for the invaders. The prompt and accurate response of the British gunners at the Redan Battery and at Vrooman's Point had inflicted casualties on the Americans crossing the river. The three boats that had drifted past the point of landing had all been hit in midstream. The frightened boatmen finally beached them in a sheltered spot on the Canadian shore below Queenston known as "The Deep Hollow". Here the soldiers limped ashore to sort themselves out as best they could and to tend their wounded. Lieutenant-Colonel Chrystie, although wounded in the hand by a grape-shot, was one of the few who managed to make his way back to the battleground and join the fight. Before the day was over, most of these Americans, between seventy and eighty in number, tamely surrendered without having fired a shot.

On the river-bank near Queenston where Colonel Van Rensselaer had landed, the Americans were also in difficulty. Major Dennis's handful of the 49th Regiment and militia were engaging them with a sharp musketry fire, and the two little grasshopper guns were pouring grape-shot at them. From near the Redan Battery half-way up Queenston Heights, Captain Williams's regulars and Captain Chisholm's militia were also firing down on the landing-place.

Colonel Van Rensselaer was hit four or five times in as many minutes and had to be helped back to the shelter of the river-bank. Here and there in the small open space between the river and the foot-path, the fallen bodies of dead or wounded Americans lay like abandoned heaps of old clothes. With their leader and three other officers wounded, the rest of the first wave of invaders gave up their attempt to form a firing-line inland and also retired behind the river-bank. Here they huddled, firing as best they could from under cover, but still suffering casualties from Williams's men above them. Until reinforcements reached the Canadian shore, the Americans appeared able to do little but wait and hope that they would not be attacked in force.

Captain Williams now led his men and the militia down from the Redan Battery to thicken Major Dennis's firing-line. With Colonel Van Rensselaer and several other officers wounded, the command of the Americans was assumed by a twenty-six-year-old captain who had never before been under fire. John E. Wool of the 13th Regiment, U.S. Infantry, was a huge man, bigger even than General Brock, for he stood six feet four inches high. On this day, Captain Wool's gigantic figure was time and again a rallying point for the American soldiers. And, in spite of his inexperience, Wool proved himself a born fighting man.

As soon as Wool saw the red-coats march down from the Redan Battery, he realized that the British had made a false move. The Heights were now undefended. If he could only reach them without being seen, he would be able to take the defenders in the rear. In an instant he made up his mind. He called for volunteers, and, with 150 men following him, made his way along the river and began to climb the escarpment from the far side. The going was very rough and at times the Americans had to haul themselves up almost vertically, clutching at outcrops of rock and small bushes. They tore their hands and ripped their uniforms, but they followed Wool grimly. Later they discovered a steep and narrow fisherman's path which had been left unguarded. Here they could stand upright and no longer had to feel that they were helpless targets if discovered. By following this path they reached the high ground above the Redan Battery. So far their presence had gone undetected.

By now it was daylight. The storm had passed with the coming of dawn and the October morning was crisp and bright when General Brock arrived at the scene of the fighting. He listened to Major Dennis's report and inspected what he could see of the battlefield from near the river-bank: the Americans were sheltering there without being able to advance but being steadily reinforced now as more and more boats crossed over, loaded with fresh men. If the whole American army succeeded in crossing the river, the British were lost, for they would be out-numbered by more than four to one.

Brock decided to visit the Redan Battery half-way up the hill to get a better view of the battlefield. When he put Alfred to the slope, the ten-year-old horse responded gallantly in spite of the hard ride from Fort George. A few minutes later Captain Wool's men in the woods above the battery saw the General's tall figure swing out of the saddle to stand beside the gun. Macdonell and Glegg accompanied the general on this reconnaissance.

The Americans at once opened fire. A hundred and fifty muskets were trained on Brock, his aides, and the twelve British gunners who were serving the eighteen-pounder. Luckily the range was too great for accurate shooting, but the musket-balls began to whistle all around Brock's little party.

Everyone looked at the General, waiting his orders. A quick glance up the hill showed Brock that he would have to retire or be captured. Wool's men were already running down towards the gun with fierce cries.

"All right, lads," Brock said, "down you go!"

The members of the gun detachment were off down the hill like rabbits. Brock turned to Macdonell and Glegg. "You too, gentlemen," he said with a smile.

The General and his aides did not take time to mount but went slithering down the slope, leading their horses by the bridles. Back at the firing-line Brock quickly decided what he would have to do. There was no sign of General Sheaffe and the Fort George garrison. Colonel Macdonell was sent back to Brown's Point to hurry up the two flank companies of York militia, but the only troops Brock could muster for an attack were Williams's company of the 49th and some militiamen, about ninety or a hundred soldiers in all. Major Dennis with the other 49th company and the rest of the militia were required in the firing-line. Yet the General knew it was vital to drive the Americans from the Heights. Unless that was done, he would be unable to mount an attack on the rapidly increasing enemy forces on the river-bank.

Without delay Brock began to form up his little group for an attack up the hill. He rode up and down the line as the men hurriedly fell in. Then, drawing his sword, he led them up against the enemy.

The red-coated soldiers gave a great cheer as they stepped out behind their General. There was no one they would more readily follow. Brock turned half around on his horse and said with a smile: "Save your breath, lads. You'll need it when we get to the top of the hill."

He was heavily outnumbered by the enemy above him, but Brock was at the head of a detachment of his old regiment, his beloved 49th, and he had every hope that he would be able to sweep the Americans from the Heights. Perhaps, too, his previous experiences of American troops caused him to underrate their fighting qualities.

At first he led the way on horseback, but when he came

to a low stone wall near the base of the hill he dismounted. Taking up his position near the left of the line and several paces in front of it, he led his men forward on foot.

The advance had not gone far when disaster overtook it. The Americans were firing from behind trees, but without much effect. A few men were hit and went down, but the line continued steadily on. General Brock himself was wounded by a musket-ball that struck his wrist, but he ignored the wound.

Then it happened. While the advancing soldiers watched in horror, they saw an American militiaman coolly step out from behind a tree not thirty yards away from General Brock. The soldier raised his musket, took careful aim, and fired. At that range and against such a target it would have been hard to miss. The musket-ball entered the General's breast and passed cleanly out through his left side. His huge figure faltered, swayed for a moment, then crumpled and fell. General Brock lay still upon the damp ground beside a small bush of wild thorn.

Brock died almost instantly, and with his death the advancing line faltered and stopped. A groan went up from the British soldiers when they saw their leader down. Two of them picked up his body and began to carry it down the hill. A moment later the entire line was in retreat.

Not long afterwards Colonel Macdonell arrived at the foot of Queenston Heights with the two companies of York Volunteers, some ninety men in all. Wild with grief and rage at the General's death, Macdonell formed up

the York Volunteers beside the regulars and militia who had retired with Brock's dead body and about nine o'clock led them up the hill in a second attack.

By now, however, Captain Wool had been reinforced.

Instead of 150 Americans on the Heights, there were 300, and they were commanded by a very brave and determined officer. Nevertheless, in spite of outnumbering the British by nearly two to one, the Americans at first fell back before Macdonell's fierce advance. They retreated past the captured Redan Battery, pausing only to spike the eighteen-pounder gun, and continued to retire up the hill. There was something very intimidating about the steady tramp-tramp-tramp of the advancing scarlet line. The Americans retreated almost to the brink of the escarpment overlooking the river before Captain Wool could get them to stand and form. An American officer hoisted a white flag, but Wool tore it down and gave orders for a final musketry volley to be followed by a charge.

That last volley wounded Captain Williams, and Macdonell's horse was shot from under him. As the brave aide-de-camp was falling, another musket-ball struck him and passed through his body. With both Macdonell and Williams down, the advancing British line wavered and halted, then broke as the Americans charged with Wool at their head.

This time the British did not stop to rally at the foot of the hill. The heart had temporarily gone out of them. They fell back and back. At the foot of the Heights, Major Dennis, although wounded in the thigh by a musket-ball, roughly bandaged himself, climbed into Alfred's empty saddle, and rode up and down on the big grey horse, attempting to collect enough men for a stand. Only a handful gathered around him, and with these he covered the retreat. The British soldiers passed through the village of Queenston and retired along the road that led to Fort George.

At Queenston, in one of the cottages overlooking the

river (legend has it that it was the cottage belonging to Laura Secord) a little group of officers and men paused long enough to deposit General Brock's body. They laid it down on the bare floor of the tiny parlour and hurriedly covered it with a pile of old blankets so that the advancing Americans would not discover what a deadly blow had been struck at the British cause that morning. Then the retreat continued.

The men were not halted and formed up again until they reached the Half-Moon Battery at Vrooman's Point. There they awaited General Sheaffe and the reinforcements from Fort George. Colonel Macdonell, in great pain from his wound, was borne back to Fort George as carefully as the rough road allowed. He knew that he was dying himself, but he spoke continually of General Brock and of what his loss would mean to Canada.

By ten o'clock in the morning the Americans were landing reinforcements, without opposition except from the single gun at Vrooman's Point which continued to fire at long range. General Van Rensselaer, dressed in civilian clothes, now crossed the river for the first time. When he heard that the British and Canadians had been driven back and General Brock killed, he believed his victory complete, but instead of quickly getting the rest of his army across he contented himself with giving orders to fortify a camp at Queenston.

Captain Wool, who had been several times wounded, at last agreed to return to Lewiston. He turned over command of the troops on Queenston Heights to Brigadier-General William Wadsworth of the New York militia.

On the hill with Wadsworth was Lieutenant-Colonel Winfield Scott, a highly competent regular officer, who in fact exercised command. By early afternoon the American forces at Queenston had been built up to well over a thousand men, although more than five thousand still remained on the other side of the river.

With Brock dead and Macdonell and many other officers wounded, the British and Canadians at Vrooman's Point were badly disorganized. They did not number more than about 250 all ranks.

At two o'clock, however, the Americans on Queenston Heights looked down and saw, some two and a half miles away, General Sheaffe's force from Fort George on the march to Vrooman's Point. From the top of the escarpment the column looked like a scarlet cord flung down across the brown and gold countryside. The sight was unexpected, for as the hours had gone by the Americans had come to think that there would be no more counter-attacks that day.

During the morning Sheaffe had received word of Brock's death and the repulse of the British forces, and this may have made him hesitate. Nevertheless, he was fortunate that he was not opposed by a more energetic commander. The battlefield at Queenston Heights was only some seven miles from Fort George, where the troops had been ordered to stand to at four o'clock in the morning; General Brock's message ordering up Sheaffe must have reached the fort by six-thirty; Colonel Macdonell's attack had not failed until nine-thirty – a good three hours after Sheaffe received Brock's order to march. And yet the

Fort George garrison did not appear within sight of the
battlefield until two in the afternoon. Van Rensselaer had
had plenty of time to get the bulk of his army into Queenston, and if he had done so, the battle of Queenston
Heights would certainly have ended very differently.

As it was, Sheaffe at least obeyed the second of Brock's
orders: he sent the Indians well out to his right as scouts
and skirmishers. The Indians, who numbered about 200,
were under the command of Chief Norton and young
John Brant, the eighteen-year-old son of the famous
Joseph Brant. Making their way across country by forest
paths, they climbed Queenston Heights from the north-
west and drove in the American outposts there.

General Sheaffe picked up the remnants of the 49th
companies and Canadian militia at Durham's Farm near
Vrooman's Point. Then, instead of marching straight for
Queenston, he turned his column west through the ham-
let of St. David's to approach the Heights from the far
side. Because the Indian attack had driven back the
American pickets, Sheaffe was able to get his force to the
hilltop almost without opposition and without any loss.

When he had seen Sheaffe's slow approach, General
Van Rensselaer had at once recrossed the Niagara River
in a belated attempt to hurry up his reinforcements. To
his astonishment, Van Rensselaer now found that the
New York militiamen refused to move. They had heard
the sounds of the battle in the morning; they had seen
their wounded return; and now, as they listened to the
faint war-whoops of Brant's Indians on the Heights, the
American militiamen decided that they wanted no part

of the fighting. Van Rensselaer pleaded with them, and wounded officers exhorted them to come to the rescue of their comrades on the Canadian shore, but the soldiers turned sullenly away, some of them claiming that when they had enlisted they had not engaged to serve outside the State of New York. The regulars in Lewiston were willing to cross the river, but the frightened boatmen refused to ferry them. General Van Rensselaer did not think it necessary to go back himself, but he did manage to send some ammunition over to Wadsworth and Scott.

There, hemmed in between the gorge of the Heights on one side and Sheaffe's army on the other, the Americans were in a desperate situation. Probably there were no more than 600 of them on the hilltop, although in and around the village below there were another 400 who did not join in the battle. Winfield Scott, finding himself suddenly attacked from the rear, did what he could. He turned his men about and arranged them in some sort of order to face Sheaffe's army. But every American soldier could see for himself that the situation was desperate. Behind them was the sheer drop of Queenston Heights and in front of them a much larger force of the enemy. A sick feeling of hopelessness was reflected in every face.

Sheaffe took his time, but the British line was drawn up by three o'clock. On the left, resting on the escarpment, were the Indians; then came a company of Negro troops from Niagara, runaway slaves who had sought freedom in Canada; and next to them the Canadian militia. The flank companies of the 49th were in the centre, and on the right was the bulk of the 41st Regiment, part of which had just arrived from Chippawa. In all, Sheaffe had about a thousand men, including his Indians.

The battle opened when the Americans made a half-hearted attempt to turn the British right by advancing across a patch of broken ground that was covered with bushes and scrub pines. They were met by such a hot fire from the 41st Regiment that they halted and turned back in confusion. Then the Indians at the other end of the line and the light company of the 41st in the centre rushed forward to form an advanced line of skirmishers. This was not a real attack, but the Americans began to give way before it. Seeing this, Sheaffe ordered the "General Advance" to be sounded. The thin notes of the bugles rang out across the escarpment, and the British and Canadian troops sent up a cheer and charged. Within seconds the entire American force was broken and in flight. Colonel Scott tried without success to rally his men; their only thought was to get away.

Behind them came the Indians with their tomahawks and the red-coats with their bayonets, chopping and stabbing whenever they caught up with the fleeing enemy. In their desperate attempt to escape, some of the invaders tried to lower themselves down the escarpment and fell to their deaths on the rocks below. Some drowned trying to swim the Niagara River. Colonel Scott, a white kerchief tied to the tip of his sword, had to fight his way through several groups of murderous Indians before he could capitulate. In Queenston village, hundreds of American militiamen were trapped when the boatmen refused to cross the river to take them off. The rounding up of prisoners took some time, but General Wadsworth formally handed over his sword to Sheaffe just as the sun was setting.

The day's fighting cost the British fourteen killed, sixty-seven wounded, twenty-one missing, as well as five Indians killed and nine wounded. The enemy's losses were harder to estimate. The Americans admitted to ninety dead and about a hundred wounded, and the British certainly captured 925 Americans, including seventy-three officers – more men than General Sheaffe had soldiers engaged.

Yet, as the Prince Regent wrote when he heard the news, General Brock's death would "have clouded a victory of much greater importance". This portion of the Prince Regent's letter was suppressed by Sir George Prevost in his order-of-the-day, possibly out of consideration for General Sheaffe's feelings.

Colonel Macdonell lived, in constant agony, for a full twenty hours after having been shot, but he died in the early morning of October 14. The British lost only two officers as a result of the battle, but those two had been the flower of the army.

The bitter news reached York the next day, and one family had a double cause for grief. Susan Shaw and her niece, Mary Powell, were together when they learned that they had both lost their lovers at Queenston Heights. Miss Shaw lived to be a very old lady but she never married.

On the 16th General Brock's body was borne slowly back to Fort George along the road he had travelled in such haste three days before. Behind the cortège marched the flank companies of the 49th Regiment with their arms reversed and with muffled drums. Alfred, fully accoutred and with empty saddle, was led by four grooms. The journey took three hours, and during all that time minute-guns along the frontier boomed mournfully. In an un-usual mark of respect to a gallant enemy, the American guns on the far shore joined in the tribute.

Major Glegg attended to the funeral arrangements, and in keeping with what he knew would have been Brock's wishes kept them as simple as possible. General Brock and Colonel Macdonell were buried side by side in the cavalier bastion of Fort George. Many brave soldiers unashamedly shed tears as the two coffins were lowered into the ground. Then from the ramparts of the fort all the guns spoke together in a final salute, and the mourners turned away.

Fittingly enough, the news of Brock's death was carried to his native island of Guernsey by the ship *Fame*. Yet glory was the least of the attributes for which Brock is remembered. His gentleness, honour, integrity, valour, and simplicity were what made him well-beloved and gave him his greatness.

The war, which lasted another two years, ended without a definite victory for either side, but Brock's life and its heroic end inspired the Canadian people with a pride and confidence they had lacked before. His achievement in the critical year of 1812 had been decisive, and not even his death could undo what had been accomplished. He had united the Canadian people in the hour of danger, and by clear strategic vision, combined with the vigour and courage to carry out bold yet simple plans, he had saved Upper Canada when all the odds were against him. If it had not been for Isaac Brock, Jefferson's prediction that the conquest of Canada would be "a mere matter of marching" might well have come true. Thus, in a very real sense, Canada's present independence is the gift of the soldier from Guernsey.

He left other gifts behind as well, most notably the love and gratitude felt for him by successive generations of Canadians. These are indeed gifts, for such emotions ennoble a people and make it in some way akin to its heroes.